"The *Mind-Body Workbook for Anxiety* is an incredibly effective res̶ ...̶ ...̶
use this program in my clinical practice as well as my personal lif̶e ...̶ ...̶
their anxiety in as little as one session. I recently worked with a c̶ ...̶ ...̶veral rapes.
Almost daily, she experienced high levels of anxiety and overwheln̶ ...̶ ...̶, and found herself shutting down in certain situations. After using the skills of mind-body bridging (MBB) for only one week, she stated, 'This has changed my life! Where was this three years ago when I really needed it? I have finally found something that works!' I have seen life-changing transformations in many clients and know this program works. Choosing to integrate MBB into your everyday practices can relieve your anxiety and change your life forever."

> —**Rachel Jenkins-Lloyd, MSN**, therapist and forensic nurse at Salt Lake Sexual
> Assault Nurse Examiners and assistant professor at Roseman University

"This *Mind-Body Workbook for Anxiety* reduces anxiety and stress within days by empowering the reader to self-heal. The mind-body mapping exercises in the book let the reader personally experience the shift from a faulty brain network to his or her natural healing executive functioning. I have witnessed the dramatic impact of using the easy-to-apply tools in this workbook personally and in my work with patients suffering from anxiety and depression. As Block says, 'Self-healing is your birthright.'"

> —**Peter D. Farr, MD**, medical director of addiction medicine, Dearborn County
> Hospital, Lawrenceburg, Indiana and member of the American Society of
> Addiction Medicine

"Mind-body bridging is brilliant in its simplicity and profound in its results. By far the most effective and easiest tool I have used both personally and professionally to achieve life-changing results. The symptoms of anxiety rapidly fade as we use our innate powers to overcome the self-defeating mind-body tug of war present in all of us. By learning and applying the simple techniques in this workbook, healing occurs spontaneously and powerfully."

> —**Maxann Shwartz, PhD**, founder of Clinical, Forensic, and Neuropsychology
> Associates of New Mexico

"Using the mind-body bridging (MBB) tools described in the *Mind-Body Workbook for Anxiety* has had a very profound impact on my personal and professional life. I use these tools regularly with my patients and there is not only a rapid relief of symptoms, but a remarkably deep transformation that empowers their lives. I strongly recommend this book to all doctors and their patients."

> —**Heli Jussila-Martineau, MD**, Helsinki, Finland

MIND-BODY WORKBOOK for anxiety

Effective Tools for Overcoming Panic, Fear & Worry

STANLEY H. BLOCK, MD
& CAROLYN BRYANT BLOCK
with ANDREA A. PETERS

NEW HARBINGER PUBLICATIONS, INC.

Publisher's Note

The information contained in this workbook is intended to be educational. The authors and publisher are in no way liable for any use or misuse of the information. The ideas, techniques, and suggestions in this workbook are not intended as a substitute for expert medical, substance abuse, or mental health diagnosis, advice, or treatment. If you are under the care of health care professionals, please consult with them before altering your treatment plan. All names and identifying information of individuals in this workbook have been disguised to protect their anonymity.

Distributed in Canada by Raincoast Books

Copyright © 2014 by Stanley H. Block & Carolyn Bryant Block
      New Harbinger Publications, Inc.
      5674 Shattuck Avenue
      Oakland, CA 94609
      www.newharbinger.com

Acquired by Jess O'Brien; Cover design by Amy Shoup; Edited by Melanie Bell

---

Library of Congress Cataloging-in-Publication Data on file

16   15   14

10   9   8   7   6   5   4   3   2   1   First printing

CONTENTS

ACKNOWLEDGMENTS

This anxiety workbook has been developed with the help of individuals suffering from anxiety. They have shared with us how they used mind-body bridging to free themselves from their symptoms and self-healed their anxiety. Although we have not specifically referenced others in the anxiety field, we appreciate their pioneering work. The clinicians from around the world using, developing, and refining mind-body bridging have our gratitude. Deserving of specific mention are the members of the International Mind-Body Bridging Certification Committee: Don Glover, Rich Landward, Theresa McCormick, Andrea Phillips, Isaac Phillips, and Kevin Webb. The research efforts of Yoshi Nakamura, David Lipschitz, and Derrik Tollefson to establish a firm evidence basis for mind-body bridging are much appreciated. Carol Ann Kent, the MBB coordinator, has ably assisted in the preparation of this workbook. The direction from the editors of New Harbinger Publications was most helpful.

INTRODUCTION

Human beings are ideally suited for anxiety. Our minds are so adept at weaving stories about past or future happenings that potential disasters are never far from our consciousness. Our nervous system is so efficient that whatever happens in our brain is immediately relayed to every organ system in our body. Worry about doing certain things or being in particular situations dominates our mind and body to such an extent that fear and avoidance control our life. Anxious thoughts—fears of losing control, past unpleasant memories, and persistent troubling impulses—make the body respond with such symptoms as palpitations, chest pain, shortness of breath, dizziness, trembling, or abdominal distress.

ANXIETY

Having anxiety can be like living with a time bomb that might go off at any minute. Intense worry, fear, or acute body distress can occur quickly and unexpectedly. Your life becomes limited as more and more energy is consumed in trying to avoid the triggers that bring on your anxiety.

Living with anxiety can mean your life is directed by an overexcited body, worrisome thoughts, and troubling behaviors that are difficult to control. There may be times you are forced to spend a great deal of time doing repetitive behaviors (hand washing, ordering, checking), which do not benefit yourself or others, in an effort to reduce your anxiety. At other times you worry excessively about everyday activities. Fears of being in particular social or public places (elevators, theaters, parties, busy stores, airplanes) cause you to avoid going places and doing many things. You may be troubled by intrusive sexual or aggressive thoughts or images. Lastly, those of you who have had past traumatic experiences may be forced to live as if the past is forever rooted in every cell of your mind and body, with any reminder of that trauma bringing forth intense anxiety. Day and night, it is impossible to get away from reexperiencing the trauma.

This workbook provides you with straightforward and easy-to-use anxiety-reduction tools that naturally settle your mind and calm your body. When you use these tools in your everyday life, you will experience your ever-present self-power, healing your anxiety. Your wellspring of healing is so powerful that even long-standing and severe symptoms respond.

IDENTITY SYSTEM (I-SYSTEM)

The holistic system that regulates mind-body states is called the "I-System." It's either active (on) or at rest (off) (Block and Block 2007; Block and Block 2010; Block and Block 2012; Block and Block 2013). The I-System is active when you are having anxiety symptoms. You know it's on when your mind is cluttered with fearful and troubling thoughts, and your body is responding with a variety of symptoms. This holistic system is called the "I-System" because when it's on, we falsely *identify with* the contents of our spinning thoughts and the resulting physical distress. It is crucial to notice the I-System, because when it's active, your body's natural way of working is disrupted. When you find yourself having any of your usual anxiety symptoms, realize that it's *always* your I-System causing the mind-body distress and preventing you from living free of anxiety. Once the I-System is active, you live your daily life as if your mind and body are your enemies. Everyday life is a struggle.

MIND-BODY BRIDGING

Mind-body bridging is an effective and easy way to put the I-System to rest and rapidly begin healing. When your I-System is calm, your mind and body are cooperating (bridging) to self-heal your panic, fear, and excessive worry. You are then free to live your best life.

Mind-body bridging, a branch of mind-body medicine, may, at first, seem similar to existing therapeutic approaches such as dialectical behavioral therapy (DBT; Linehan 1993), cognitive-behavioral therapy (CBT; Beck 1995), acceptance and commitment therapy (ACT; Hayes, 2005), mindfulness-based stress reduction (MBSR) (Williams et al. 2007), and other therapy approaches. However, recent research (Tollefson et al. 2009; Nakamura et al. 2011; Nakamura et al. 2013) and clinical experiences demonstrate that mind-body bridging is unique because its therapeutic effect is very powerful and has a very rapid onset (within the first week). Research has also shown that mind-body bridging quickly reduces an anxiety and stress biomarker, alpha-amylase (Lipschitz et al. 2013).

In mind-body bridging the major premise is that we are always connected to a wellspring of healing, goodness, and wisdom. The reason for your painful symptoms is that when the I-System is active, it keeps you from reaching your personal wellspring of healing. As you quiet your I-System, you can begin healing your anxiety symptoms.

BRAIN BASIS

Brain research (Weissman et al. 2006) has found two networks of functioning with different features: an executive network and a default-mode network. The *executive network* coordinates moment by moment how we see the world, think, make decisions, and act. It's responsible for the direction and management of our lives. The *default-mode network* is at work when we're having exaggerated thoughts about ourselves and our experiences, making it difficult to respond appropriately to situations as they come up. Researchers have found that when the default-mode network is active (on), the executive network is inactive (off) (Boly, Phillips, Balteau et al. 2008). Only one network can be in the driver's seat at a time.

Using fMRI, scientists and doctors can now take pictures of how the brain changes while it's busy. Shaun Ho (Block, Ho, and Nakamura 2009) suggests that the I-System refers to the default-mode network, and that mind-body bridging refers to the executive network. Brain research (Boly, Phillips, Tshibanda et al. 2008) shows that when the default-mode network is not active (off), your executive network takes charge (on), regulating your mind so that you function at your best. The I-System is why all your efforts to date have not resolved your most difficult anxiety symptoms. Mind-body bridging quiets the I-System, letting you heal and function naturally in the executive mode.

Imagine a big switch in your brain that turns the I-System (default-mode network) on and off. When the I-System is on, it shuts down your executive functioning and makes you prone to anxiety. When the switch is off, you function at your best, heal your anxiety, and access your wellspring of healing, goodness, and wisdom.

MIND-BODY LANGUAGE

Your mind and body do not function without each other; they work as a single unit that you can't separate (the *mind-body*). You will learn a clinically validated mind-body language that allows you to know, connect with, and manage your mind and body as never before. This easy-to-understand language frames your mind-body states in terms of an active (on) or inactive (off) I-System. With this awareness you gain the power to quickly start reducing your symptoms and to start healing your anxiety.

There are times when your anxiety flares up. Your head is full of fearful and troubling thoughts, your body is full of tension and symptoms, and you can't see the light at the end of the tunnel. This state of mind and body is the *powerless self*. The powerless self is not simply a mental state; it also affects every cell of your body. It's caused by the activity of your I-System, not by your thoughts or circumstances. This powerless self puts you in a box and prevents you from accessing your healing power.

This workbook is based on the fact that your *mind-body* (mind and body as a unified whole unit) can heal your anxiety and allow you to live your best life. This mind-body state is your natural *powerful self* that always functions in the executive mode. When you use the tools in this book, you will soon find that you come to a state of natural harmony and balance in your life, where your mind and body naturally work together. Each chapter lists the new mind-body language used in that chapter.

HOW TO USE THIS BOOK

This workbook has powerful, easy-to-do exercises to help you heal your anxiety. In chapter 1—Use Your Senses to Reduce Anxiety—you will discover the root cause of your anxiety. Then you can rapidly experience and apply your new, easy-to-use tools in your everyday life to reduce your anxiety. In each following chapter you continue to develop, use, and personalize the effective tools through the simple *Discover, Experience, and Apply* method. Every chapter serves as a building block for the next one. It is important to do the exercises and read each chapter in sequence so you can create a solid foundation to move forward in healing your symptoms. As you move through the chapters, your list of self-healing tools keeps growing, so that you can rely on them for anything that's going on in your life.

You will find an MBB (mind-body bridging) Quality of Life Gauge at the beginning, middle, and end of the book, which will help you to measure how your life changes. At the end of each chapter there is an MBB Rating Scale that lets you know how well you're using the self-healing tools you are learning. When you use your tools in your life every day you'll reduce your symptoms and self-heal your anxiety.

CHAPTER 1

USE YOUR SENSES TO REDUCE ANXIETY

Discover, Experience, and Apply

Discover how the I-System causes your anxiety.

Experience how tuning in to your senses reduces anxiety.

Apply your anxiety reduction tools in your daily life.

Mind-Body Language

I-System: Each of us has an I-System, and it's either active (on) or resting (off). When it's on, it creates anxiety. You know the I-System is on when your mind is cluttered with spinning thoughts, your body is tense, your awareness contracts, and your mental and physical functioning is impaired. It's called the I-System because it prompts you to falsely identify with the spinning thoughts and the physical distress it causes.

Powerful self: How you think, feel, see the world, and act when your I-System is resting. Your powerful self always functions in the executive mode where your mind and body work in harmony, as a healing unit.

Mind-body bridging: When you use the tools in this workbook, you form a bridge from your active I-System, which can cause anxiety flare-ups, to your powerful self in the executive mode, which handles daily life in a smooth and healthy way.

DISCOVER THE CAUSE OF YOUR ANXIETY

Let's get started so you can discover the cause of your anxiety. Think of a situation (for example, being in a crowd) that makes you anxious. Write it in the oval below. It may be helpful to look at the sample map on the next page. Now, take a couple of minutes to write down around the oval any thoughts that come to mind about that situation. Be as specific as possible. Work quickly without self-editing.

SITUATION THAT MAKES YOU ANXIOUS MAP

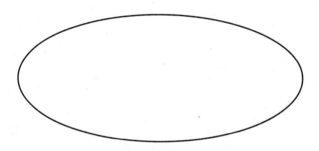

A. Is your mind clear or cluttered with thoughts?

_____

B. Is your body tense or relaxed? List where and how your body is tense:

_____

_____

C. With your mind and body in this condition, how do you feel and act?

_____

You probably think it's the situation that's creating the inner distress and anxiety you see on your map. It's not! You have just experienced your active I-System. Your I-System takes a particular situation, creates mind clutter and body tension, and limits your ability to act without anxiety. The next map will show you that it's not the situation that's causing your anxiety. It will also teach you the critical first step in anxiety reduction.

SAMPLE MAP: SITUATION THAT MAKES YOU ANXIOUS

No exit

Can't breathe

Hate to be closed in

You never know what
people will do.

Crowds are dangerous.

BEING IN A CROWD

There are so many
stories about people
getting crushed.

Thinking about being in
a crowd is making my
heart race.

A. Is your mind clear or cluttered with thoughts?

My mind is cluttered with anxious thoughts about being in a crowd.

B. Is your body tense or relaxed? List where and how your body is tense:

Band around my head, hard to breathe, really tense all over.

C. With your mind and body in this condition, how do you feel and act?

Anxious—avoid crowds at all costs.

EXPERIENCE HOW TO REDUCE ANXIETY

The next part of this exercise can change your life forever, because it shows you the cause of the anxiety and how to reduce it. For this important map, it's helpful to be in a room without distractions such as people talking, TV, or electronic devices. Write that same situation (the one you wrote in the oval on the first map) in the oval below. Before you continue, seat yourself comfortably, listen to any background sounds, feel the pressure of your body on your seat, feel your feet on the floor, and feel the pen in your hand. Take your time. If you have thoughts, gently return to listening to the background sounds and tuning in to your senses. Once you feel settled, start writing whatever comes to mind about the situation. Watch the ink go onto the paper, keep feeling the pen in your hand, and listen to the background sounds. Write for a couple of minutes.

SITUATION THAT MAKES YOU ANXIOUS MAP WITH BRIDGING

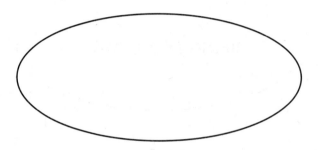

A. Is your mind clear or cluttered with thoughts?

_____

B. Is your body tense or relaxed?

_____

C. How is this map different from the first one you made?

_____

If this second map is not different, find a quiet room, and take your time as you follow the above instructions while you do the map again.

D. How would you feel and act in this mind-body state?

_____

E. If you could live your life with your mind-body in this state, do you think your life would be better?
Yes _____   No _____

The exercise you just did is called *...body mapping.* These important two-part mind-body maps ... minutes. Mapping is a snapshot of your thoughts and level ...

... two completed maps. Your first map shows your I-System ... what it's like to have a quiet I-System. You experienced that ... using on your body sensations and the sounds around you, ... tension eases, and your anxiety reduces. Mind-body bridg- ... from a place where you are anxious and restricted to your ... node. Remember, your powerful self is how you think, feel, ... resting.

... ll of anxiety and worry and didn't have enough room left ... you quiet your I-System, as you did in the second map, you ... e situations in a healthy way (as shown in figure 1.1 on the ... nged. When you have troubling thoughts and anxiety, you ... d that you can only use a small portion of your executive ... -System, you become a bigger vessel. Your space to manage ... n mind-body bridging so that your powerful healing state ... e to deal with life's challenges is exactly how mind-body ... ng situations quickly and in a healthy way, without anxiety ... ing executive functioning builds naturally. Keep in mind ... ion naturally; this skill will develop on its own. It is your

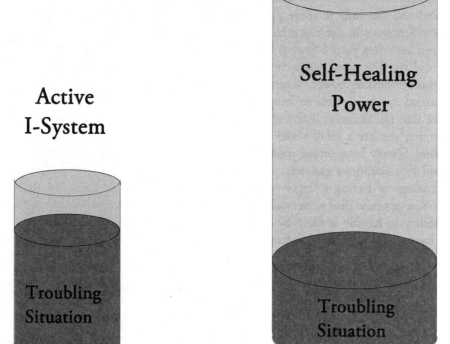

Figure 1.1 Which vessel are you in?

When you feel anxious, you see yourself as a small and limited vessel. Your ability to handle troubling situations (the darkly shaded space) is greatly reduced. You have falsely come to believe that the small vessel is all you are. This allows you to only use a fraction of your self-healing power (lightly shaded area). When your I-System is active, you feel limited and stuck. This stops you from being able to manage your anxiety.

You automatically become a bigger vessel when the I-System is resting. The situation hasn't changed, but the space inside the vessel has changed. The lightly shaded area in the larger vessel (which refers to your self-healing power and your ability to manage anxiety) expands as you switch off your I-System.

MBB QUALITY OF LIFE GAUGE

Date: _____

It's time to fill out your first MBB Quality of Life Gauge. This scale is repeated throughout the workbook so that you can measure the impact that this book has on the quality of your life. Think back over the past week as you fill out the chart.

Circle the number under your answer.	Not at all	Several days	More than half the days	Nearly every day
1. I've had positive interest and pleasure in my activities.	0	1	3	5
2. I've felt optimistic, excited, and hopeful.	0	1	3	5
3. I've slept well and woken up feeling refreshed.	0	1	3	5
4. I've had lots of energy.	0	1	3	5
5. I've been able to focus on tasks and use self-discipline.	0	1	3	5
6. I've stayed healthy, eaten well, exercised, and had fun.	0	1	3	5
7. I've felt good about my relationships with my family and friends.	0	1	3	5
8. I've been satisfied with my accomplishments at home, work, or school.	0	1	3	5
9. I've been comfortable with my financial situation.	0	1	3	5
10. I've felt good about the spiritual base of my life.	0	1	3	5
11. I've been satisfied with the direction of my life.	0	1	3	5
12. I've felt fulfilled, with a sense of well-being and peace of mind.	0	1	3	5

Score Key:

Column Total ____ ____ ____ ____

0–15 . . . . Poor

16–30 . . . . Fair   Total Score _____

31–45 . . . . Good

46 and above . . . . Excellent

ANXIETY REDUCTION TOOLS

Remember the mapping exercise? When you did the first map, you explored a situation that made you anxious. The second map allowed you to explore that same situation with a calmer body and clearer mind. Maybe this state lasted for a while, or maybe it was brief. When you made your second map, what pulled you away from hearing the background sounds, feeling the pen, and seeing the ink go onto the paper? Yes, it was your thoughts. The I-System spins your thoughts, makes your body tense, and closes you off from your senses. It converts troubling situations into inner distress and anxiety. Thought labeling and bridging awareness practices are the tools you will learn in this chapter to help you reduce your anxiety.

Thought Labeling

Your mind naturally makes both positive and negative thoughts. You will never get rid of your negative thoughts. In fact, trying to get rid of them doesn't work, because when you push them away, you give them even more energy, adding to your anxiety.

When troubling thoughts come up, it helps to label them using an anxiety reduction tool called *thought labeling*. Thought labeling lets you see that a thought is *just a thought*. This prevents the I-System from taking a thought, spinning a story from it, crossing the mind-body connection, and creating an anxiety-filled body. Once that happens, the thought is no longer just a thought, but a state of mind-body distress.

Let's see how thought labeling works. Recall a thought that upsets you; for example, *Did I make sure the door is locked?* Since the thought causes anxiety, it means your I-System captured that thought. The thought has become boss, and you have become its servant. When that tension-filled thought pops into your mind, say to yourself, *I'm having the thought, "Did I make sure the door is locked?"* Some people even continue with *and a thought is just a thought*. This recognition that a thought is just a thought is one of the tools that will help you stop your I-System from capturing thoughts. When the I-System doesn't grab your thoughts, your powerful self in the executive mode handles the situation without excess anxiety.

Sara, a thirty-five-year-old mother and highly respected massage therapist, seemed to have it all together. But her racing mind about "what could go wrong" was creating excessive worry about problems at home and at work, and was starting to interfere with her ability to supervise her staff at the spa. A friend suggested she try mind-body bridging. Sara found that thought labeling quieted the spin of her I-System and reduced her worrying. She blogged, "Mind-body bridging taught me to be in control of my thoughts, and it changed my life." Now when she has the thought, *What if the clients stop coming*, she labels it as *I'm having the thought, "What if the clients stop coming?", and a thought is just a thought*. Sara's marriage and relationship with her children, as well as her ability to supervise the staff at the spa, improved dramatically.

Use thought labeling to reduce your anxiety. During the day, when anxious thoughts pull you away from what you are doing, label the thoughts and go back to your activity. For example, when you're in the shower and the thought *I will never get through the day* pops into your mind, say to yourself, *I am having the thought, "I'll never get through the day,"* return to taking your shower, sense the water on your body, and hear the sounds of the shower.

Bridging Awareness Practices

When the I-System is active, it closes off your senses until all you are aware of is your anxiety. It's like putting your hands over your ears to block out any other sound. The I-System not only keeps you from hearing the background sounds around you, but also keeps you from experiencing your ever-present self-healing powers. When you use your senses, your I-System quiets, letting you deal with your challenges with a calm, ready mind and a relaxed body.

Bridging awareness practices use your senses to build a bridge from a life filled with anxiety (run by the powerless self of the I-System) to a life lived at its best (run by the powerful self of executive functioning). Building this bridge is easier than you think.

One rainy evening, Jeff, a Vietnam War veteran with a history of PTSD, was taking care of his grandchildren. He got an emergency call that his elderly father had just had a severe heart attack and he needed to get to the hospital right away. Jeff hated driving in heavy rain, especially at night, because it reminded him of the torrential rains in Vietnam. Feeling that he had no choice, he loaded the grandkids in the car and started driving. His mind began filling with racing thoughts, and the pressure in his chest made it difficult to breathe. Using his mind-body bridging practices, he began to actually feel the steering wheel in his hands, which helped him relax his grip. He listened to the sound of the engine, felt the road vibrations, and paid attention to the road. At the end of his trip, even the sound of the rain didn't agitate him. He told us, "My bridging awareness practices saved my life and my grandchildren's."

AWARENESS OF BACKGROUND SOUNDS

Your environment is full of sounds. During the day, pause and listen to any background sounds, like the white noise of the heating or air-conditioning system, the wind blowing, traffic sounds, or the hum of the refrigerator. If your thoughts start to spin, label them and gently return your awareness to what you were doing. See what happens to your mind and body when you focus on background sounds.

Lynnette, twenty-eight years old, was referred to a mind-body bridging therapist by the battered women's shelter where she was staying. She had not only been a teenage runaway from an abusive home, but had lived on the streets for several years before entering an abusive marriage.

When she walked into the therapist's office the first time, she was guarded and full of mistrust. As the interview started, she became anxious, stated she could not breathe, and began to cry and shake. At this point her therapist knew very little about her, but asked her if she would listen to the sounds in the office for a moment. Lynnette did so reluctantly, and within a minute, she closed her eyes, her breathing slowed, and the tears stopped. She continued listening until she became calm. When asked to open her eyes, she said, "What did you do? I feel calm for the first time in ages!" Her therapist explained that she had done nothing but help her to rest her cluttered mind and tense body. As therapy progressed, Lynette learned to rest her active I-System and had fewer and fewer anxiety attacks. When she did have an attack, Lynnette was able to bring herself out of it quickly, by using her anxiety reduction tools.

AWARENESS OF WHAT YOU ARE TOUCHING

We all touch hundreds of things every day. Were you aware of how it felt under your fingertips today when you touched your shoes, socks, shirt, keys, fork, watch, paper, cell phone, or computer? Were you aware of your senses when you touched your child or a close friend? Did you sense the warmth of the coffee cup or the coldness of the water bottle in your hand? Chances are you didn't. Your I-System has numbed your body, detaching you from your senses. Tuning in to your sense of touch is another bridging awareness practice that quiets your I-System and strengthens your self-healing power.

Be aware of what the sensations are like under your fingertips as you touch things like glasses, phones, pens, keys, computers, and other objects. Are these surfaces smooth or rough, cold or warm, pleasant or unpleasant? When washing your hands or showering, feel the water as it touches your skin. Sense what it's like to touch others or be touched. This may take some effort, because the I-System dulls your senses. A young, highly stressed student told us that simply sensing his thumb rubbing against his finger calmed him down enough to stop him from getting anxious while in class.

Note what you touch and the sensations you feel during the day. Do you feel more settled when you are aware of what you are touching? Keep practicing!

AWARENESS OF COLORS, FACIAL FEATURES, AND SHAPES

The I-System grasps at certain images while rejecting others. This prevents you from seeing the whole picture. When you use one or more of your senses, the I-System calms down, your awareness expands, and you actually see what's out there. When you look at a sunset or even a speck of dust on the floor, does your busy head let you see its colors, shapes, and uniqueness? Probably not for long. Take a look at your next meal. When your food is in front of you, really look at it before you eat. What textures are there? What are the shapes? What color is your food?

Jerry, a high school junior, had had problems taking any kind of test since the third grade. He would get so uptight about taking an exam that even though he studied and knew the subject well, he would fail the test because his mind would always go blank. Jerry had tried every method his parents and teachers could come up with to help with his "exam anxiety." Nothing worked until he discovered mind-body bridging. He learned the bridging awareness practices. When taking a test, Jerry would see the color of the wall and the pattern of the tile on the floor, feel his fingers as they touched the computer keyboard, and sense his behind on the chair. He also listened to the background sound of the heating and air conditioning system in the room. Then, when a negative thought popped into his mind, Jerry labeled it as just a thought. He found that even though taking an exam wasn't fun, he didn't have the paralyzing anxiety which had caused his brain to freeze.

Pay attention today to what you see when you look at scenery and objects. Notice their colors, shapes, and forms. Pay attention to the facial expressions of the people around you: family, friends, coworkers, and even strangers. When you have an anxious thought, label it as just a thought and gently return to whatever you were doing. When you really see what's out there, your I-System quiets, and your appreciation of life expands as your anxiety fades.

AWARENESS OF YOUR BODY

Awareness of how your body feels is an important part of your ability to self-heal anxiety. Because of the unpleasant body sensations associated with your anxiety, you may have developed a habit of trying to block out or get away from the feelings in your body. You may get away from those unpleasant feelings for a little while, but avoiding your body sensations prevents your self-healing of anxiety. When you have unpleasant body sensations, expand your awareness to all parts of your body and pay particular attention to background sounds and the sensations of the things you touch. Your expanded awareness means you have expanded your self-healing powers.

The proprioception system is a vital part of your nervous system that informs you about your posture, the way you move, and the degree to which your muscles contract. The tense muscles you noticed when you did your first map were due to the I-System getting in the way of the natural functioning of the proprioception system. Your natural functioning is signaling for the muscle to relax, but your I-System takes over that normal response and tightens up the muscle even further. This is an example of how the I-System works to disrupt mind-body harmony. Another example is responding to an injury that causes pain. The acute pain is a signal to take action right away. After a few minutes, the central nervous system sets up a barrier to reduce the pain signals so that you are better able to carry on with your daily life. In many people with chronic pain, the I-System removes the barrier so that the intense pain remains for weeks, months, or even years, getting in the way of their daily lives and things they need to do.

Let's see how this works. Start leaning slowly to the left. Do you feel the muscle tension in your side? Do you sense the imbalance in your head? Do you sense how your natural functioning wants to correct the imbalance? Lift up your right arm and hold it in midair. Do you feel the pull of gravity? Yes, that's your proprioception system at work. It gives you information about the position of your body in space and the state of your muscles. You use that natural flow of information to automatically move and navigate. Pay attention to gravity as you lift an object or as you get up from a chair. Gravity is your friend; it's always there. Sensing gravity quiets the I-System and grounds you in the present moment.

Fran loved to run and entered several marathons every year. After learning mind-body bridging, she applied the bridging awareness practices to her running. She was able to reduce her time in events by fifteen minutes without having to spend more time training. Here is how she did it. At the beginning of the race, instead of worrying about the heat, the course, or her training, she would feel her feet on the ground, hear the background sounds, and would sense her pulse and breathing slowing. When climbing a hill, Fran would feel and hear each foot hitting the ground. Rather than forcing herself to speed up or slow down, she would let her body be the guide naturally. At the top of the hill, she was amazed at how relaxed and ready to continue running she felt. After a while she began to experience some new training issues involving her right leg. By having a new awareness of her body, Fran observed a breathing pattern of only her right foot touching the ground when she exhaled. With bridging, she developed a natural breathing rhythm so that she could alternate which foot would hit the ground when she exhaled. This new awareness eliminated the problems she was having with her right leg. As Fran continued to use mind-body bridging, the wear and tear on her body during training lessened and her time continued to improve.

APPLY THE TOOLS IN YOUR DAILY LIFE

Use your anxiety reduction tools to manage your anxiety, stay relaxed, and stay focused throughout the day. When your thoughts begin to wander from what you are doing, label them as just thoughts and then bring your attention back to the activity. When you first start to feel anxious, or have unpleasant body sensations (as you did on the first map), use your bridging awareness tools. Notice how your body automatically relaxes and your breathing becomes natural without your having to force it. You are now in direct communication with your mind-body. For example, while you are cooking, listen to the stove's exhaust fan, and you will find that your other senses automatically open. You smell the soup, you see the colors of the vegetables, and your sense of calm expands.

Roger, suffering from bouts of shortness of breath and limited physical activity due to chronic obstructive pulmonary disease (COPD), started to become fearful and anxious whenever he had problems breathing. He read about mind-body bridging and quickly discovered that it made sense to him and could help him with his anxiety. Now Roger uses his anxiety reduction tools to control his anxiety when he is short of breath. He listens to background sounds, listens to the sounds of his breathing with his portable oxygen device, feels the fabric of his clothes, sees the objects that are around him, and senses the gravity when he moves. He found that his ability to be active has actually improved by feeling his feet on the ground. When he has thoughts about not having enough air, he labels his thoughts, and is calmed by the sound of his oxygen device. The quality of Roger's life has greatly improved.

As you are falling asleep tonight, listen to and focus on background sounds. Feel and rub the sheets with your fingers. See the darkness when your eyes are closed. Be patient and keep returning to your senses. The busy head can never settle the busy head. If anxious thoughts (*I have to meet new people tomorrow*) keep you awake, label your thoughts; for example, say to yourself, *I'm having the thought, "I have to meet new people tomorrow"* or *I'm having the thought, "I hate meeting new people, so what else is new?"* and then return to your senses and fall asleep. These anxiety reduction tools (using your senses and thought labeling) stop the activities of the I-System from robbing you of a restful sleep. The quality of your sleep is an important component in reducing anxiety. Improving sleep using mind-body bridging is very effective (Nakamura et al. 2011; Nakamura et al. 2013).

Anxiety Reduction Tools

➢ Recognize when your I-System is active (on) or inactive (off).

➢ Thought labeling

➢ Bridging awareness practices:

- Awareness of background sounds

- Awareness of what you are touching

- Awareness of colors, facial features, and shapes

- Awareness of your body sensations

You may ask yourself, *Can labeling my thoughts, listening to background sounds, seeing facial features, feeling my feet on the ground, and being aware of what I touch really help me reduce my anxiety and live a better life? Can it really be so simple?* When you make a habit of using these tools for reducing anxiety, all the cells in your body will give you a resounding yes! So, feel your foot as it touches the ground, sense your fingers on the computer keys, hear the background sounds, feel the pressure on your behind as you sit, feel the fork in your hand, look at your food, and be aware of how the broom moves the dust when you sweep. When your troubling thoughts pull you away from what you are doing, label them and return to the activity.

After using these tools for a couple of days, return to this page. Fill out the following chart, and then the MBB Rating Scale that is on the next page.

Difficult Situation	I-System: Active or Inactive	Thought Labeling	Bridging Awareness Tools	What Happened
Thinking about the crowded concert while I was showering.	*Active*	*I'm having the thought that the crowd will crush me.*	*Paid attention to the sounds of the shower.*	*Tension dropped; I was able to calmly get ready.*

Have you noticed that besides reducing anxiety, using these tools as part of your daily routine helps you to enjoy life more and be more productive? These tools for reducing anxiety serve as the basis for the entire workbook. The stronger your mind-body bridging practices, the easier it will be to manage your anxiety. The following MBB Rating Scale is a way to gauge your progress that lets you know how solid your foundation is.

MBB RATING SCALE: USE YOUR SENSES TO REDUCE ANXIETY

Date: _____

After using the tools in this chapter for several days, check the box below that best describes your practice for each question: hardly ever, sometimes, usually, or almost always.

How often do you...	Hardly Ever	Sometimes	Usually	Almost Always
Listen to background sounds?				
Sense the sensations in your fingers when holding your water bottle, coffee cup, a cold glass of water, or a soda can?				
Sense the sensations in your fingers when you touch things throughout the day?				
Experience pressure on your feet when you walk?				
Experience pressure on your behind as you sit?				
Feel the steering wheel, hear the roar of the engine, and pay attention to the road when you are driving?				
Hear the water going down the drain and feel it on your body when you shower or wash your hands?				
Become keenly aware of daily activities like making the bed, eating, brushing your teeth, and lifting?				
Become aware of your body sensations when you touch others?				
Become keenly aware of others' facial expressions?				
Use anxiety reduction tools to help you manage situations at home and at work?				
Use bridging awareness and thought labeling tools to help you sleep?				
Use anxiety reduction tools to reduce anxiety?				
Sense that you are connected to your own wellspring of healing, goodness, and wisdom?				
Know when your I-System is active (on) or inactive (off)?				

List two new things you've noticed about your life after starting to use your anxiety reduction tools:

_____

_____

CHAPTER 2

START SELF-HEALING ANXIETY BY RECOGNIZING REQUIREMENTS

Discover, Experience, and Apply

Discover how requirements prevent your self-healing.

Experience how recognizing requirements helps you self-heal.

Apply your anxiety reduction tools in your daily life.

Mind-Body Language

Requirements: Thoughts made into mental rules by your I-System that tell how you and the world should be in each moment. When your I-System rules are broken you become fearful and full of anxiety.

Recognize requirements: When you become clearly aware that *your requirement*, not the events around you, is making your I-System active, you function in the self-healing executive mode.

HOW THE I-SYSTEM WORKS

A lot of systems regulate our bodies. For instance, we have a system that regulates our temperature, keeping the body at around 98.6 degrees Fahrenheit. If our temperature goes up, we sweat, and if it goes down, we shiver as our system tries to get back to the body's normal temperature. In the same way, we all have an I-System. It works like the system that regulates our temperature, but instead of an ideal temperature, the I-System creates an "ideal picture" (requirement) of how you and the world should be. Each moment, both systems sense whether their requirements are met. When the requirement of the system that regulates temperature is not fulfilled, we shiver or sweat. When something comes up that doesn't fulfill the I-System requirement, our I-System becomes active, and we have body tension, mind clutter, stress, and a tough time controlling our anxiety.

The natural state of the I-System is to rest. It's only turned on when requirements are unfulfilled. Remember, requirements are rules that your I-System has created for you about how you and the world should be at any moment (for example, *I should be able to control my anxiety*; *I shouldn't have intrusive thoughts*; *My partner should be more understanding*).

It's vital to know the difference between thoughts that are natural expectations and those that are made into requirements. All thoughts are natural and start free of the I-System's influence. It's not a thought's content but what happens to the thought that makes it a requirement. For example, *I don't like to shop when there are lots of people in the store* is a thought or expectation you may naturally have. The I-System works by taking that natural thought and creating an ideal picture of how you and the world should be (*few people in the store when shopping*). To do that it takes the natural thought and turns it into a requirement: *I shouldn't shop when there are lots of people in the store*. You can tell it's a requirement because you have excess body tension and mental stress whenever the situation violates the rule or demand of the requirement. When a thought is not a requirement, you still have your natural expectation, but your mind is clear, your body is relaxed, and your powerful self is in charge of your shopping experience. You are now better able to deal with anything that may come up.

It's crucial to continually recognize whether or not your I-System is active. For example, during a holiday party, a friend makes a negative comment about your clothes. Your thoughts might be: *She was cruel. Why did she embarrass me? Why did she do that?* You immediately tense up all over, your face gets red, and you find a corner to hide in. These are signs of an active I-System that's been turned on by the requirement, *My friend shouldn't make negative comments about my clothes*. When the I-System takes control of the natural thought or expectation, *My friend shouldn't make negative comments about my clothes*, it becomes a requirement. Your level of anxiety rises, impairing your ability to enjoy the party. Even after your friend leaves, your mind remains cluttered with thoughts, and your body is still tense. Your I-System pours salt on the wound by continuing to spin your thoughts and by tensing your body, creating even more anxiety and resentment. Your I-System could continue to spin stories about the incident and your distress could fill the entire holiday season. It's important to notice that whenever the I-System captures a natural thought or expectation and makes it into a requirement, you become a victim of circumstances because your ability to act free of anxiety is handicapped. This chapter gives you the tools to quiet your I-System, regain your executive functioning, and self-heal your anxiety.

DISCOVER HOW REQUIREMENTS PREVENT SELF-HEALING

It's time to start mapping your I-System requirements. Remember that the two-part mind-body maps are short written exercises that take only a few minutes. They're vivid pictures of your thoughts and body tension. Every two-part map you create makes you more aware of your requirements, reduces control by your I-System, and helps you to self-heal your anxiety.

This mapping exercise is a powerful way to uncover requirements that sap your ability to live your best life. Do a "How My World Should Be" map (see the following sample map). Take a few minutes to write around the oval any thoughts that you have about how your everyday world should be; for example, *My partner should understand what I am going through*, or *I shouldn't be afraid*. Be specific and work quickly without editing your thoughts.

HOW MY WORLD SHOULD BE MAP

HOW MY WORLD SHOULD BE

SAMPLE MAP: HOW MY WORLD SHOULD BE

I shouldn't have those
recurring troubling thoughts.

I shouldn't be afraid.

Everything should be in order.

My partner should understand
what I am going through.

I should be in control.

HOW MY WORLD SHOULD BE

My parents should have gotten
me the help I needed.

The house should
be the way I like it.

I shouldn't worry about germs.

I should plant a flower garden.

My family should accept
me as I am.

A. Do you think everything on your map will happen?   Yes _____   No _____

B. In this chart, write down each thought and describe your body tension when you realized that it might **not** happen.

"How My World Should Be" Thought	Body Tension and Location	
Example 1: *My family should accept me.*	*Churning stomach, palpitations*	√
Example 2: *I should plant a flower garden.*	*Minimal body tension*	

C. The body tension you listed is a sign that the thought is a requirement and has activated your I-System. Place a check mark in the third column to indicate that the particular thought is a requirement.

We all have natural thoughts about how the world should be. When your I-System takes hold of these thoughts and you see that they might not happen, your body tenses and your mind gets cluttered. This sets the stage for you to experience anxiety.

Remember, thoughts that turn on your I-System are requirements. In the previous example, take the thought, *My family should accept me.* When you have the thought, *My family should accept me*, your stomach churns, your heart pounds, and your thoughts spin. This means you have the requirement, *My family should accept me*, and your requirement is interfering with your natural ability to cope with that thought in a healthy way. If your I-System hadn't captured that thought, it would have remained a natural expectation. You would then relate to your family with a relaxed body and a clear mind whether or not your family accepts you. For the other thought listed as an example (*I should plant a flower garden*), you have minimal body tension when reality (no flower garden) doesn't match that thought. In that case, your I-System is not triggered, so the thought *I should plant a flower garden* isn't a requirement, it's a natural thought from executive functioning. It means that you'll still have a relaxed body and a clear mind whether or not you plant a flower garden.

START TO EXPERIENCE HOW TO SELF-HEAL ANXIETY

Now you'll use the bridging awareness practices you learned in chapter 1 and do a How My World Should Be map again. Before you start writing, listen to any background sounds, experience your body's pressure on your seat, sense your feet on the floor, and feel the pen in your hand. Take your time. Once you feel settled, keep feeling the pen in your hand and start writing about how your world should be. Watch the ink go onto the paper, and listen to any background sounds. For the next few minutes, jot down whatever comes to mind about how the world should be.

HOW MY WORLD SHOULD BE MAP WITH BRIDGING

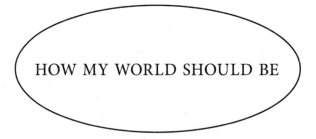

A. What are the differences between this map and the previous map?

_____

_____

B. Do you see that you can face your world as it is, without having the extra pressure of your I-System, as is shown on the previous map you made?   Yes _____   No _____

When something happens in your life (*My house isn't in order*) that fills your mind with spinning anxious thoughts and tenses your body, you know it's your I-System, not the condition of your house, that makes you feel distressed. If you recognize your requirement and tune in to your senses, you will quiet your I-System. Your mind clutter, body tension, and anxiety will soon reduce so you can handle what's happening with a ready, relaxed mind and body.

RECOGNIZE REQUIREMENTS DAILY

Whenever you have body tension (unpleasant body sensations) and mind clutter (troubling anxious thoughts), it's a sign that one of your I-System requirements is not being fulfilled and you may be on the edge of experiencing anxiety. The mapping exercise you just did is about increasing your awareness of your requirements. Notice your signs of an active I-System. For example, maybe your shoulders start to rise, your stomach churns, you feel overwhelmed, you stop hearing the fan, or you slump in your chair. Once you notice a sign, see if you can find the requirement that activated your I-System. When you identify your requirement, you have more control over what's upsetting you. Remember, it is not the situation or another person's behavior that activates your I-System; it's your own requirement.

Mull over the upsetting situations you have had in the past few days, and fill out the chart.

Situation	Mind Clutter	Body Tension	Requirement
Go into a public restroom.	It's dirty, I'll get sick, I can't do it.	Head spinning, body shaking	I shouldn't have to go into a public restroom.
Drive in heavy traffic.	I'll have an accident, can't control bad drivers.	Chest pressure, short of breath	I shouldn't have to drive in heavy traffic.

Go back over each requirement you listed on the chart. Use your bridging awareness practices and thought labeling, and see if you have less stress and anxiety. Using your anxiety reduction tools puts your powerfulself back in charge.

Ann, a college student, would spend hours anxiously getting ready to go to class. Even when her homework was done, she was so anxious about being prepared and well-dressed that she would miss class. Getting high grades did little to reduce her anxiety about attending classes. Her life changed completely after being introduced to mind-body bridging. Using anxiety reduction tools, she labeled her thoughts and tuned in to her senses to calm her I-System. She became aware of her footsteps while walking to class, the way the door felt when she opened it, the change in temperature as she entered the building, and the way her behind felt as she sat on her chair during class. Mind-body mapping let her recognize her requirements, *I should look attractive* and *I should be perfectly prepared*. Labeling those thoughts and listening to the background sounds reduced her anxiety. Ann now attends class regularly without experiencing anxiety.

WHAT UPSETS ME

The unexpected is just around the corner, filling life with situations that could upset you. Doing mind-body mapping prepares you to face those situations without melting down. In this exercise you work with a current situation that could lead up to experiencing anxiety. In the first map you identify the requirements connected to the situation. The second map lets you feel the mind-body shift from an active I-System to an I-System at rest. Mapping reins in your anxiety and allows you to function in a natural way in the executive mode.

1. Do a What Upsets Me map. In the center of the oval, write down a current situation that upsets you. Next, take a couple of minutes to write around the oval any thoughts that come to mind. Work quickly, without editing your thoughts. At the bottom of the map, carefully describe the areas of your body that are tense.

WHAT UPSETS ME MAP

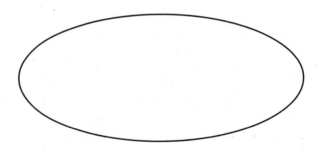

Body Tension: _____

_____

Recognizing the start of the tension in your body is a basic first step in managing your anxiety. Your body always has tension or negative body sensations before your anxiety becomes full-blown.

What does your map say about how you are approaching the situation?

A. Is your mind cluttered or clear?

_____

B. How would you feel and act in this state?

_____

_____

_____

Recognizing your requirements is crucial to managing your anxiety. Look at what you wrote in the oval (for example, *Driving in rush hour traffic*) and discover your requirement (*I shouldn't have to drive in rush hour traffic*). Do the same for each item on your map (*It makes me anxious*) and uncover your requirement (*It shouldn't make anxious*). This skill of recognizing your requirements can change your entire life.

C. List all the requirements from your map:

_____

_____

_____

_____

_____

_____

When you are not aware of your requirement (*I shouldn't have to drive in rush hour traffic*), your I-System is kept active. You can only have anxiety when your I-System is active. The key to reducing anxiety is to be aware of the progression of your body tension and then recognize your requirement. Once your I-System quiets, your mind and body settle down on their own.

2. Use the same situation from the previous map, and do a bridging map using your bridging awareness practices. Write the situation in the oval. Before you start writing, listen to any background sounds, feel your body's pressure on your seat, sense your feet on the floor, and feel the pen in your hand. Take your time. Once you feel settled, keep feeling the pen in your hand, and start writing. Watch the ink go onto the paper, and listen to any background sounds. Take a couple of minutes.

WHAT UPSETS ME MAP WITH BRIDGING

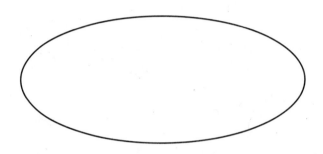

A. Is your mind cluttered or clear?

_____

B. Is your body tense or relaxed?

_____

C. In this mind-body state, how would you feel and act?

_____

D. What are the differences between the two maps?

_____

_____

You can do two-part maps whenever you feel anxious to help you uncover the requirements that are creating your anxiety. When you quiet your I-System, your anxiety lessens. No matter what you are thinking, anxiety is not possible with a relaxed body. Mapping is a critical tool for you to self-heal your anxiety.

BEFRIEND YOUR BODY

1. Befriending your body is a mind-body bridging tool that is vital for managing your anxiety. The location, type, amount, and buildup of body tension (chest pressure increasing) on the first What Upsets Me map are clear-cut signals that when you have tension in that area of your body, your I-System is active. You are now in danger of experiencing anxiety. Go back to the first What Upsets Me map and fill out the chart using the items that are filled with the most tension.

What Upsets Me	Body Sensation	Behavior	Requirement
My son didn't come home by curfew.	Tight chest, gets hard to breathe	Cried when he got home.	He should be home by curfew so I know he's safe.

2. Using your mind-body bridging tools, as you did on the What Upsets Me map with bridging, you experienced a release of body tension. This is your executive mode's natural state. Fill out the below chart using the information you listed on the bridging map.

What Upsets Me	Body Sensation	State of Mind	Behavior
My son didn't come home by curfew.	Breathing settles down	Concerned	Called him and reminded him of his curfew and asked him to come home.

Using your anxiety reduction tools throughout the day keeps you aware of your body's signals. It's important to notice the first signs of body tension because when you don't, your body tension and discomfort can increase. Then your mind spins wildly with troubling thoughts until your body is all worked up and a full-blown anxiety attack occurs. It's critical that you recognize the early signs of body tension and troubling thoughts, and start using your anxiety reduction tools right away.

3. What anxiety reduction tools are working best for you? List them:

_____

_____

_____

TRIGGERS

Another important method of improving your ability to manage anxiety is to examine triggers. A *trigger* is an event or thought that activates a requirement, heating up your I-System. Any event or thought is a trigger if, and *only* if, that event violates a requirement. Every coin has two sides, and even when flipped, it's still the same coin. Triggers and requirements are the same way. When you become aware of a trigger, it's important to realize that it's pointing you to the requirement (the other side of the coin). Remember, it's not the event, thought, or someone else's behavior that activates the I-System; it's your requirement about that event, thought, or behavior.

Carol was raised in an isolated community. In her extremely violent home, it was forbidden to talk about what went on; therefore there was no one to help her. After she grew up and moved away, Carol was plagued with severe anxiety attacks that would happen whenever there was any conflict among coworkers, neighbors, or family. This triggered a pounding heart that would skip beats, uncontrollable trembling, and tears. She felt guilty for not being able to control these responses. Carol tried avoiding conflict and angry people, and she obsessively cleaned to try to reduce her anxiety. Behavior therapy was somewhat helpful, but many of her symptoms were unchanged. Her sleep continued to be disrupted, and she would awaken with anxiety. After she learned mind-body bridging, Carol recognized her triggers and the ways her body signaled that her I-System was active (pounding heart, skipped beats, trembling, and tears). She uncovered her requirements related to her triggers (angry neighbors, critical brother, gossiping coworkers, etc.), and was able to use her anxiety reduction tools to live her best life. Carol reports that she hasn't experienced anxiety for several years, and that she deals with conflict calmly, in a healthy way.

Life is full of events that upset you, make your I-System active, and create inner distress that drains your emotional resources. When you clearly recognize the triggers (events or thoughts) that switch on your I-System, they will not upset you as much as before. When someone's actions toward you stir up your anxiety (for example, your husband is cold toward you), it helps to ask yourself, *What does that trigger behavior look like?* Some answers might be *His loud voice, His hard facial expression,* and *The words he uses.* Next, look for your hidden requirements that go with each trigger action (*He shouldn't raise his voice, His face should be relaxed,* and *He should use kind words*).

Let's get up close and personal with your triggers. Take a few minutes to do a Triggers map by jotting down what triggers your I-System, such as the way others act or events that happen (for example, *Staying home alone, Going shopping, Not checking the stove*).

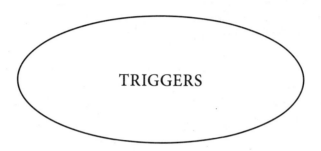

Choose the items from your map that are most likely to make you anxious. List these triggers, your associated body tension, and the underlying requirement. Mind-body mapping is always about your I-System requirements, not someone else's behavior. Remember that the trigger points to your requirement.

Trigger	Body Tension	Requirement
Staying home alone.	Heart pounding, band around my head	I shouldn't have to be home alone.
Not checking the stove.	Shoulders raise and then get tighter	I should check the stove often.

USE YOUR BODY AS A COMPASS

Throughout the day, be aware of your body tension, especially those areas of your body that were tense on your Triggers map. Although the I-System causes body tension and creates anxiety in your life, it's no more your enemy than a friend who is giving you vital information. Being aware of the early signs of body tension lets you know when you are heading in the wrong direction (toward an anxiety buildup). Use these signals as you would a compass (figure 2.1). When you notice that the I-System is on, know that you are off course. This is when you use your anxiety reduction tools to quiet your I-System, and your executive functioning will put you back on the right course.

Cindy, a state government worker, had received positive job reviews for the past fifteen years. Her new supervisor felt that anyone older than a certain age, who had worked at their job for longer than five years, was no longer an asset. No matter how hard Cindy tried to meet the demands of her supervisor, her work was never "good enough." She became very anxious about going to work, and started having health issues—migraine headaches and IBS (irritable bowel syndrome). Cindy dreaded the weekly meetings where her supervisor would persistently grill and embarrass her in front of the whole group. After starting mind-body bridging, she began using her body as a compass. Whenever she began to feel tension in her gut and tightness in the back of her neck, she would immediately use her bridging awareness practices to relieve the tension. By mind-body mapping she became aware of two requirements (*I should be perfect* and *I should get positive feedback from my boss*). She used thought labeling every time these requirements would come up, and her anxiety reduced further. Cindy also discovered that when she was in her natural functioning executive mode, she could clearly see that the unreasonable demands of her supervisor would never change, and that working harder and longer was useless. With this new understanding and continuing to use her body as a compass, Cindy's headaches and her bouts of IBS became very rare. She realized that this job was no longer a good fit for her, and transferred out of the department.

Many times your I-System's mind clutter keeps you from knowing how your body feels, and this sets the stage for experiencing anxiety. Like Cindy, note your first signs of body tension. These first signs are a red flag that your anxiety symptoms are starting to build. The earlier you are aware of the process, the easier it will be to prevent anxiety attacks. Being aware of how your body responds is a crucial mind-body bridging tool. Use your body as a compass (befriend your body) to create mind-body balance in which you are in control of your life. Remember, when your body is tense and your mind cluttered, your I-System is in the driver's seat. To quiet your I-System, use your anxiety reduction tools by noting your body tension; recognizing that it's your requirement, not what's happening, that's causing your anxiety; and then listening to any background sounds, sensing whatever you're touching, and going back to your executive functioning.

Headache   Muscle Aches

Tightness

Tension

Clear Headed   Calm

Flexible   Relaxed

Figure 2.1 Use your body as a compass.

A bird that migrates has an inner compass that tells it when it's veering off course on its way home in the spring. When you notice your I-System in action, it becomes your compass, letting you know when you are off course. Being aware calms your I-System and shifts you into natural executive functioning. This puts you on course to deal with your daily life without anxiety.

ANXIETY-DISSOLVING MAP

1. When you are feeling anxious and it's hard to find the underlying requirements, do a What's on My Mind map. Take a couple of minutes to write whatever pops into your mind around the following oval. Work quickly, without editing your thoughts.

WHAT'S ON MY MIND MAP

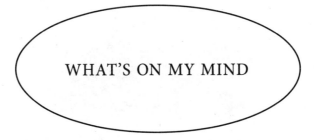

A. Is your mind cluttered or clear?

_____

B. Describe your body tension:

_____

_____

This is a momentary snapshot of what's on your mind. Notice which thoughts are connected to body tension (for example, *My daughter is acting out, I have to go to the store, My car is getting old*). Recognize the requirement in each thought (*My daughter shouldn't act out, I shouldn't have to go to the store, I should have a new car*).

C. What are your requirements?

_____

_____

_____

2. Do this map again, this time using your bridging awareness practices. Before you start writing, listen to any background sounds, feel your body's pressure on your seat, sense your feet on the floor, and feel the pen in your hand. Take your time. Once you feel settled, keep feeling the pen in your hand, and start writing. Watch the ink go onto the paper, and listen to any background sounds. For the next few minutes, jot down whatever thoughts pop into your mind.

WHAT'S ON MY MIND MAP WITH BRIDGING

Observe the differences between the two maps:

_____

_____

Remember, thought labeling helps. For example, if you have the thought, *My life could be ruined*, say to yourself, *I'm having the thought, "My life could be ruined."* What is ruining your life right here, right now, isn't losing your job, but the thoughts your I-System has spun about losing the job. You don't have to fix your thoughts, push them away, or force any changes. When the I-System is at rest, your powerful self in the executive mode will automatically help you make decisions about your course of action without the I-System clouding your mind. During the day, being aware that *A thought is just a thought* is all it takes; then you can return your awareness to the task at hand.

APPLY THE TOOLS IN YOUR DAILY LIFE

To get in touch with and express your healing powerful self, use your mind-body bridging awareness practices every day. When you do, even a slight increase in jitteriness will remind you to use your anxiety reduction tools, and you'll go back to being your powerful self in the executive mode.

Angela, a salesperson for a large software company, enjoyed her job and was proud to be the company's top salesperson. Not long ago, Angela came in second in sales and was devastated by her "failure" to be number one. She began to doubt herself and worried more and more about her performance. This led to her getting sick to her stomach, breaking out in a sweat, getting dizzy, and shaking as she prepared to make a sale. She had lost her confidence, no longer enjoyed her job, and saw herself as a failure. Angela began mind-body bridging and by using her anxiety reduction tools, she started to deal with her anxiety. She used the two-part mind-body mapping tool to find her requirements:

I shouldn't let the company down.

My sales skills should always be the best.

I should be the top salesperson.

I should always be calm and cool.

I should never show emotions.

While mapping Angela reported, "It's not about my performance, the customers, or even the company; it's my requirements that are causing my anxiety!" She began using her body as a compass to tell her when her I-System was beginning to activate, and she was able to stay in the executive mode more and more. With a quiet I-System, Angela was now able to recognize her requirements as they came up in her daily life, and soon her anxiety symptoms subsided, and she truly enjoyed her sales job.

Mind-body bridging is an ongoing practice. Use your anxiety reduction tools to live every aspect of your life with a calm I-System. Your new tools from this chapter are listed below.

Anxiety Reduction Tools

➢   Create two-part mind-body maps every day and again whenever you begin to feel anxious.

➢   Discover how requirements activate your I-System.

➢   Recognize requirements to quiet your I-System.

➢   Use your body as a compass by befriending your body.

MBB RATING SCALE: START SELF-HEALING ANXIETY BY RECOGNIZING REQUIREMENTS

Date: _____

After using the tools in this chapter for several days, check the description that best matches your practice for each question: hardly ever, sometimes, usually, or almost always.

How often do you...	Hardly Ever	Sometimes	Usually	Almost Always
Locate and recognize body tension as a sign of an overactive I-System?				
Notice the destructive effects that the I-System has upon your life?				
Notice that an overactive I-System is underlying your anxiety?				
Recognize your requirements?				
Catch yourself drifting away from being present in the moment?				
Use bridging awareness practices to quiet the I-System and improve the quality of your life?				
Come to appreciate your life in a different light?				
Do a daily two-part mind-body map?				

When your I-System is active, how do you deal with your anxiety?

_____

_____

When you are using your anxiety reduction tools and your I-System is quiet, how do you deal with difficult situations?

_____

_____

What's the most important benefit of doing two-part mind-body maps?

_____

CHAPTER 3

TAKE CHARGE OF YOUR DEPRESSOR AND SELF-HEAL

Discover, Experience, and Apply

Discover how your depressor stops you from managing your troubling thoughts and sets the stage for your anxiety symptoms.

Experience how taking charge of your depressor helps you manage your troubling thoughts and allows you to self-heal.

Apply your anxiety reduction tools in your daily life.

Mind-Body Language

Powerless self: How you think, feel, see the world, and act when your I-System is active. Life is overwhelming, your executive functioning is impaired, and you struggle to control your anxiety.

Depressor: A part of the I-System that takes your natural negative thoughts and self-talk (things you say to yourself) and creates body tension and mind clutter. It makes you feel weak, powerless, and vulnerable, setting the stage for your anxiety symptoms.

Storyline: Thoughts that your I-System spins into stories (true or not) that keep your I-System going, create anxiety, and pull you away from what you are presently doing.

Defusing the depressor: When you become clearly aware that your negative thoughts are "just thoughts," you reduce the power of the depressor. This allows your mind-body to start healing from the mental and physical distress (anxiety) caused by the I-System.

THINKING AND NEGATIVE THOUGHTS

Did you know that from the viewpoint of neuroscience, a thought is just a secretion, a droplet of chemical at the synapse where two brain cells connect? Did you know that psychologists and others who study the mind sometimes call thoughts *mind facts*? These mind facts are organized, stored, and used as needed to deal with events as they come up. In this chapter you will learn how your I-System takes hold of your thoughts and makes it hard for you to manage your anxiety.

It is vital to know how your mind thinks and uses thoughts. If you have the thought *high*, there must be a *low*; if you think *good*, there must be a *bad*; and the same follows for *happy* and *sad*, *calm* and *angry*, *sick* and *well*, and *young* and *old*. The mind works with both positive and negative thoughts. Most of us struggle over what to do with our negative thoughts. Many people try to use positive affirmations to get rid of or deal with their negative thoughts. We have all tried to fix ourselves with positive affirmations, but when we stop, the negative thoughts come back with a vengeance. So what do we do about negative thoughts? Have you noticed that pushing them away only gives them more energy? For example, try not to think of a red balloon. What are you thinking of? A red balloon! The only time we will get rid of our negative thoughts is when we're brain-dead.

So the question remains: What do we do with negative thoughts? The natural powerful self functions in the executive mode, creating harmony and balance out of opposite thoughts. For instance, happiness and sadness are emotions that we all have. Your powerful self knows how to deal with each. But the I-System has a much different approach. Its mission is to keep itself switched on by grabbing thoughts, usually negative ones. The *depressor*, a part of the I-System, works by taking your negative thoughts and self-talk, and creating body tension and mind clutter that results in anxiety. It takes a negative thought like *I'm a loser*, *I can't cope*, or *I'm no good*, and weaves a story about that thought, filling every cell of your body with negativity and anxiety. You see yourself as powerless, broken, or ruined, and you have a story and a body full of anxious tension to prove it! This mind-body state is known as the *powerless self* and is behind your anxiety. Some people with anxiety try to deny or cover up their negative thoughts; however, when you deny or are unaware of your negative self-talk, it makes you feel even more powerless. The mental and physical distress caused by the I-System's depressor is one of our main reasons for not self-healing anxiety; so it's very important to be clearly aware of your negative thoughts and feelings about yourself.

The original question, *What do I do about my negative thoughts?*, now becomes *What do I do about my depressor?* The depressor is the doom and gloom of your I-System. It uses the negative self-talk that naturally occurs during the day to make you feel weak and powerless. Today you'll begin to see your negative self-talk for what it is, just thoughts. This is another crucial step in your becoming able to stay in the executive mode and avoid anxiety.

David had a successful career and a loving, supportive wife, but his negative, self-critical talk was beginning to ruin his life. His negative self-talk included: *I'm not organized enough*; *I cause my headaches because I can't sleep*; *If I relax, I'll mess up*; *I don't eat right*; and *I'm afraid I'll say the wrong thing*. David's body tension and spinning thoughts were creating insomnia and stomach problems. This negative self-talk was affecting his interactions with others because of his negative focus. All this I-System activity had him anxious and depressed. A colleague at work recommended mind-body bridging. After learning the bridging awareness and thought labeling tools, whenever a negative thought would pop up (*I can never get it right*), he would label that thought (*I am having the thought, "I can never get it right"*), come to his senses, and return to what he was doing. David learned about his I-System's depressor and how it captured natural negative thoughts and embedded the negativity into his body. David began doing depressor maps and learned how his I-System was making him feel victimized and weak. His outlook began to change as he mapped daily and used his anxiety reduction tools whenever he recognized that his I-System was active. Now, when a negative thought pops up, after he labels this thought as just a thought, he adds a lighthearted *So what else is new?* and goes about his day.

Try hard to recall your negative self-talk from the past twenty-four hours. On this chart, note your thoughts, the kind of body tension you have, where it's located, and how it is related to your anxiety symptoms. Notice how your negative thoughts are related to your level of body tension.

Negative Self-Talk	Body Tension
I'm not a good person, nothing I do is good enough, I'll give up trying.	*Sweating, building pressure in chest, and its getting harder to breathe*

Recognizing your negative self-talk may not, at first, seem to be directly related to your specific anxiety symptoms. Some people have even said that their negative self-talk is due to their inability to cope and control their anxiety symptoms. But what we have discovered is that when your depressor is in control of your negative thoughts, it will continue to create so much mental and physical chaos that your anxiety keeps growing. The secret to preventing your negative thinking from turning into anxiety is to know how the depressor works, how it fills your body with anxiety, and how it stops you from self-healing. The next maps will give you more tools to unlock the healing ability of your powerful self.

DISCOVER HOW THE DEPRESSOR STOPS YOU FROM MANAGING YOUR TROUBLING THOUGHTS

1. Do a Depressor map. Around the oval, write any negative thoughts and self-talk you have when you're disappointed with yourself or bummed out. If any of the thoughts are positive, see if you can find their negative opposites and jot them down (see the sample map on the next page). Write as much as you can for a couple of minutes.

DEPRESSOR MAP

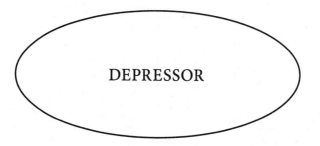

A. Describe your body tension and how it progresses:

_____

B. What's your behavior like when your depressor is active?

_____

_____

C. Describe the impact on your health and quality of life when your depressor is active:

_____

The thoughts on your map are natural thoughts that happen to be negative. The depressor works by grabbing a natural negative thought and embedding the negativity in your body. This process creates a heavy mental and physical burden that prevents healing and reinforces your anxiety.

SAMPLE MAP: DEPRESSOR

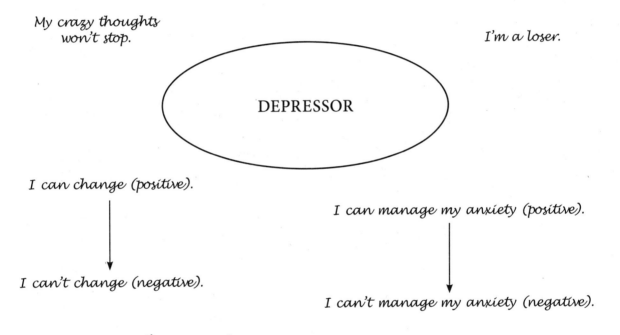

Nothing seems to help my anxiety.

My family doesn't understand my problems.

I can't do things right.

My crazy thoughts won't stop.

I'm a loser.

DEPRESSOR

I can change (positive).

I can manage my anxiety (positive).

I can't change (negative).

I can't manage my anxiety (negative).

I'm worn out.

A. Describe your body tension and how it progresses: *Tight shoulders, heavy body. The more negative my thoughts, the more my shoulders rise and the heavier my body feels.*

B. What's your behavior like when your depressor is active? *I first keep to myself, and then the worrying thoughts overwhelm me and I end up not being able to do anything.*

C. Describe the impact on your health and quality of life when your depressor is active: *I'm tired all the time, I can't sleep, and I isolate myself.*

2. Time to look at your depressor more closely. From your previous Depressor map, take the thought that troubles you the most by creating a lot of body tension (for example, *My crazy thoughts won't stop*), and write it in the following oval. Now, for the next few minutes, write around the oval any thoughts that come to mind. Use phrases or complete sentences like *Nothing I do works*, *Why me?*, or *It's hopeless.*

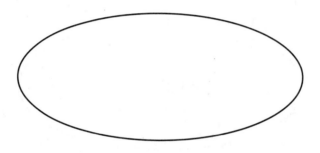

TROUBLING THOUGHT FROM MY DEPRESSOR MAP

Describe your body tension and how it progresses:

_____

_____

The map you just did holds the key to managing your depressor. The thoughts on your map are spun into stories (true or not) by your I-System. Think about the stories that come to mind about your negative thoughts. Remember, these are called "storylines." It's very important to recognize and become aware of how they control you. Storylines are the link between the negative thoughts that pop into your mind, the mind-body distress you experienced on your last two maps, and your anxiety symptoms. The I-System's spinning storyline takes a natural negative thought and embeds the negativity into every cell of your body. Storylines keep the I-System going, taking you away from the present moment. Stopping the depressor's storylines keeps negative thoughts from creating a painful mind-body state that leads to anxiety.

3. Start to experience how to manage your troubling thoughts. Use your bridging awareness practices and do the previous map again. Write the same troubling thought in the oval. Before you continue, listen to background sounds, feel your body's pressure on your seat, sense your feet on the floor, and feel the pen in your hand. Take your time. Once you feel settled, keep feeling the pen in your hand and start writing. Watch the ink go onto the paper, and listen to background sounds. Write for a couple of minutes.

TROUBLING THOUGHT FROM MY DEPRESSOR MAP WITH BRIDGING

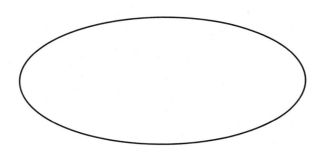

Notice the differences between the two maps:

A. Is your mind cluttered or clear?

_____

B. Is your body tense or relaxed?

_____

C. In this mind-body state, how do you act?

_____

_____

STEPS TO DEFUSE YOUR DEPRESSOR AND CONTINUE SELF-HEALING

When you feel weighed down by your troubling thoughts and have body tension or signs of anxiety, your depressor is active. Use the tools below to defuse your depressor and let your powerful self get back in the driver's seat:

1. *Recognizing the depressor*: When you observe that your mind has negative thoughts *and* your body has tension, know it's your depressor—not the thoughts, what's happening, or other people—that is causing your distress.

2. *Thought labeling*: Thought labeling is the first tool you use to control your troubling thoughts. From one of your maps, choose a thought that still creates body tension. Say slowly to yourself, *I am having the thought* _____ [insert your thought]. Are you sensing a reduction of body tension? Remember, it's your depressor, not the content of your thoughts, that causes your distress.

3. *Bridging awareness practices*: If you still feel body tension after using the steps above, listen to background sounds, and feel your behind on the chair and your feet on the floor. Do you experience less body tension? If so, you are defusing your depressor.

Joyce went to a Catholic school and had wanted to be a nun since she was twelve years old. However, while in college, she met someone she cared deeply about. She was extremely happy, but had thoughts like, *I'm not a person of faith, I'm a bad Catholic, I deserve to feel guilty because I fell in love.* When her boyfriend proposed, instead of being happy, Joyce felt even more guilty and became anxious. She couldn't choose between becoming a nun and marrying her boyfriend. The more she thought about it, the more her anxiety grew. Her grades started slipping, she couldn't sleep, and she was paralyzed about making the "right" decision. No matter how much she prayed about the situation, she felt no answer coming; she felt empty, emotionally drained, and alone. Joyce decided to go on a retreat with a woman's group. One of the leaders at the retreat was a mind-body bridging counselor. During the retreat, Joyce spent time learning about mind-body bridging, started using the anxiety reduction tools, and mapped out her dilemma. Joyce became aware of the requirements she had for herself, her faith, and being in love. As she defused her requirements, she discovered that what she really wanted was to be a teacher. Although she admired the nuns at her Catholic school, being a nun and living a nun's life was not the path she wanted to take. With a quiet I-System, she reaffirmed her faith and accepted her boyfriend's proposal.

STORYLINE AWARENESS SETS YOU FREE

Another powerful tool for reducing your anxiety is storyline awareness. Remember, storylines are thoughts spun into stories that keep your I-System active. Storylines aren't just stories; they have a harmful physical effect on your body, and cloud your mind. The negative storylines tend to define us, and the positive ones tend to confine us. All storylines keep you living in the past or dreaming of the future. This takes you away from being present in the moment and handling what's happening right now with your powerful self in charge. Storyline awareness is simply noticing the storyline, seeing the damage it's doing, and letting your awareness stop the story. Your executive functioning is restored without your even trying.

Joe, who grew up in an emotionally unstable home, was referred to mind-body bridging by his doctor for colitis, anxiety, and depression. As a child, he had become so anxious over his family situation that he had developed colitis and couldn't speak or eat in front of other people. Through mind-body bridging, he learned how to label his troubling thoughts and used the bridging awareness practices to get through his day. Using additional anxiety reduction tools, he became aware of his requirements and their storylines about himself, his family (especially his father), and growing up in a volatile home. He learned that his storylines about his angry, bitter father (who took every opportunity to ridicule him) and his passive, anxious mother (who didn't stand up for him) were keeping his depressor going, creating even more anxiety. Joe began to see that these storylines were trapping him. As he continued to recognize his requirements and storylines, Joe's childhood became a past memory. He now knows that memories are just thoughts, and *a thought is just a thought.* Joe is living his life in the present moment without being troubled by anxiety or colitis. He is no longer that anxious little boy, but a man who no longer allows the past to interfere with the present.

By using your storyline awareness tool (just being aware of the storyline) during the day, you'll see how much of your time storylines swallow up. You don't need to push the story away; you just need to become aware of it. Your awareness dissolves the storyline and will even help you sleep better at night.

As a child, Karen was afraid of getting her vaccination shots. She would get so anxious about going to the doctor that she would break out in a sweat and have the "shakes." Karen was diagnosed with adult-onset diabetes and had to learn to give herself insulin injections. Being afraid of needles, this situation created even more anxiety. Her mind began spinning with thoughts and storylines about how much needles hurt, how her mother had diabetes and Karen had watched her give herself shots every day, how bruised her mother was from the injections, and how she died of complications. She told the doctor that giving herself injections wasn't something she could do. The doctor referred her to mind-body bridging. Karen, knowing that her health depended upon having the insulin injections, began to use the bridging awareness practices and thought labeling to quiet her I-System. As she mapped out her fear about needles, Karen realized that her negative storylines and requirements were keeping her frozen in the past and fearful of the future, and were currently interfering with her giving herself injections. Now, when it's time for her to give herself insulin, she becomes aware of her storylines (even the positive ones about how she is strong and capable) and listens to the traffic sounds or fan noises. She senses her body as it moves while she prepares the injection. Using her anxiety reduction tools, Karen is now able to give herself the insulin injections without anxiety. Did they "cure" her dislike of getting an injection? No, but mind-body bridging has made it possible for her to take care of her own health care.

Thinking back over the past week, observe how your I-System created negative storylines filled with tension. Note the body tension that came with the situation, and find your hidden requirement. Fill out the chart below:

Situation	Negative Storylines	Body Tension	Requirement
Leaving home.	The doors might be unlocked; someone will rob me; I didn't check every door.	Start sweating, feel heart beating harder	I should check and double check all the doors in the house to be safe.
She criticized me.	I'll never be good enough for her.	Band around my head, jaw tight, grinding my teeth	She shouldn't criticize me.

Start mulling over one of your most distressing storylines and try to keep it going. Now, become aware of background sounds. While continuing to listen to those sounds, observe how your storyline unfolds. Is the storyline running out of gas? Continuing to use your bridging awareness practices weakens your storylines. If you still have a troubling thought (*I didn't lock the door*), label the thought (*I'm having the thought, "I didn't lock the door"*) and realize that it's not the possibility of an unlocked door that is causing your anxiety. Once a thought is captured by the I-System, you're prevented from dealing with that thought or situation in a healthy way. When you realize a thought is just a thought and a story is just a story, the thought will be powerless to create anxiety. You will be free to deal with all of your thoughts with your powerful self in charge.

MANAGE YOUR "WHAT IFS"

1. The following maps take a look at those "what ifs" that create anxiety whenever you think about them or even try not to think about them. Do a What If map. Take a couple of minutes to write around the oval any "what if" thoughts that come to mind about important situations in your life that may have a negative outcome (see the sample map on the following page). Work quickly, without editing your thoughts.

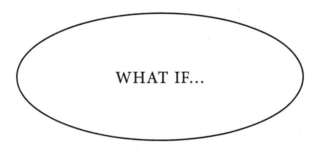

WHAT IF MAP

WHAT IF...

A. Describe your initial body tension and how it progresses to anxiety:

_____

_____

B. List your depressors and storylines:

_____

_____

C. List your requirements:

_____

_____

D. In this mind-body state, how do you act?

_____

SAMPLE MAP: WHAT IF

*...my children have
anxiety problems?*

...I get bitten my the neighbor's dog?

*...this workbook
doesn't help me?*

*... I can't find a job
that pays better?*

*...my mother doesn't
recover from surgery?*

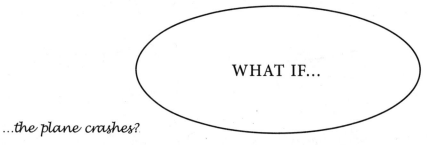

WHAT IF...

...the plane crashes?

...I never get over my terrible thoughts?

...there is a bad earthquake?

*...I die during the
next panic attack?*

...I'm gone, what will happen to the kids?

A. Describe your body tension and how it progresses: *Started with a knot in my stomach, but the more I go over the "what ifs," the more my whole body tenses up and I end up urgently needing to go to the bathroom.*

2. Use your bridging awareness practices and do the map again. Before you begin to write, listen to background sounds, feel your body's pressure on your seat, sense your feet on the floor, and feel the pen in your hand. Take your time. Once you feel settled, keep feeling the pen in your hand and start writing. Watch the ink go onto the paper, and listen to background sounds. Write for a couple of minutes.

WHAT IF MAP WITH BRIDGING

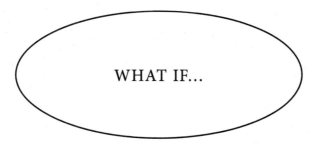

WHAT IF...

Notice the differences between the two maps:

A. Is your mind cluttered or clear?

_____

B. Is your body tense or relaxed?

_____

C. In this mind-body state, how do you act?

_____

_____

D. Are you more likely to successfully heal your anxiety in this mind-body state than on the previous map?   Yes _____   No _____

RESOLVE YOUR MOST DISTRESSING "WHAT IF"

1. Most of us have an underlying "what if" that makes us sick to our stomachs whenever we think about it (*What if I have to fly? What if I can't breathe?*). Do another map using any "what if" that creates body tension and could lead to experiencing anxiety. Write the item in the oval. Next, take a couple of minutes to write around the oval any thoughts that come to mind. Work quickly, without editing your thoughts.

MOST DISTRESSING WHAT IF MAP

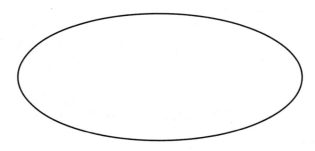

A. Describe your body tension and how it progresses:

_____

_____

B. List your depressors and storylines:

_____

_____

C. List your requirements:

_____

_____

D. In this mind-body state, how likely are you to have anxiety?

_____

2. Using your bridging awareness practices, do the previous map again. Write the same troubling item in the oval. Before you continue, listen to background sounds, feel your body's pressure on your seat, sense your feet on the floor, and feel the pen in your hand. Take your time. Once you feel settled, keep feeling the pen in your hand and start writing. Watch the ink go onto the paper, and listen to background sounds. Write for a couple of minutes.

MOST DISTRESSING WHAT IF MAP WITH BRIDGING

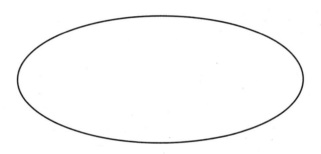

Notice the differences between the two maps:

A. Is your mind cluttered or clear?

_____

B. Is your body tense or relaxed?

_____

C. In this mind-body state, how likely are you to have anxiety?

_____

KEY QUESTIONS TO PUT YOU IN CHARGE OF YOUR TROUBLING THOUGHTS

Answer the following questions when your troubling thoughts are getting you down:

1. What are the signals that your depressor is active (*heavy body, knot in stomach, thoughts that I'm not good enough or that I'm going to have anxiety*)?

    _____

2. What is your behavior like when your depressor gets you down (*overeat, call my partner to calm me down, go to bed*)?

    _____

    _____

3. How is the depressor getting in the way of your executive functioning (*I'm not making good decisions, my parenting is inconsistent, I can't do my job, I feel a lot of pressure to fix how I feel*)?

    _____

    _____

4. Do you experience yourself as losing control of your life?   Yes _____   No _____
    How so?

    _____

5. What are your storylines (*I'll never get better, my anxiety is because of what I went through*)?

    _____

    _____

6. Are these thoughts and storylines creating who you are?   Yes _____   No _____
    How so?

    _____

7. What are your requirements (*I shouldn't have bad thoughts, I should be over my anxiety*)?

    _____

    _____

Your depressor sets the stage for anxiety by capturing your natural negative thoughts. This makes you feel weak and powerless and interferes with your self-healing.

APPLY THE TOOLS IN YOUR DAILY LIFE

Kate, a college freshman, began to skip classes and isolate herself a few weeks after the start of her first semester. The demands of college, and being away from her supportive parents for the first time, made her feel anxious and depressed. Anxiety about her body image pushed her to spend more time in the gym and to eat less. She finally sought help because she had trouble sleeping, wasn't eating, worried constantly about her how her body looked, and missed class. Within days of using her bridging awareness practices to sleep, Kate was waking up more refreshed. During the day, her awareness practices made her feel less anxious. She clearly saw how the depressor created body tension when it grabbed onto thoughts like *I'm fat*, *I'm ugly*, and *I'm not smart enough*. Kate learned to use thought labeling to keep her negative thoughts from creating mind clutter and unpleasant body tension. She saw that her storylines took up most of her day and prevented her from going to class. Mapping helped her recognize her requirements about body image and getting good grades. Using all of her anxiety reduction tools, Kate was able to make better decisions and adjust to college.

Let's look at the anxiety reduction tools Kate used.

1. She used her bridging awareness tools to calm her I-System and gain access to her innate self-healing powers.

2. She recognized it was her depressor and not her negative thoughts that was making her feel bad.

3. She used thought labeling to get control of her troubling thoughts.

4. She became aware that the spin of her storylines pulled her away from the present moment.

5. She was able to recognize her requirements, shift into executive mode, and succeed in college.

Below are the three new tools discussed in this chapter. Use them with the tools you learned in the previous two chapters to defuse your depressor, access your powerful self, and continue to self-heal your anxiety.

Anxiety Reduction Tools

➢   Recognize the depressor's activity.

➢   Become aware of your storyline.

➢   Defuse the depressor.

MBB RATING SCALE: TAKE CHARGE OF YOUR DEPRESSOR AND SELF-HEAL

Date: _____

After using the tools in this chapter for several days, check the description that best matches your practice: hardly ever, sometimes, usually, or almost always.

How often do you...	Hardly Ever	Sometimes	Usually	Almost Always
Notice negative self-talk and body tension as a sign of the depressor?				
Notice that your depressor is running wild and making you feel weak and powerless?				
Experience that the powerless self comes from your I-System?				
Recognize that an active depressor sets the stage for anxiety attacks?				
Defuse your depressor by staying aware of what it is doing and using thought labeling?				
Recognize storylines?				
Recognize your self-healing power when your I-System is quiet?				

List the body tension that comes along with the depressor and how it progresses:

_____

List the themes of two storylines:

_____

_____

List two behaviors that are connected with the depressor:

_____

_____

What's it like to defuse your depressor and live with a quiet I-System?

_____

CHAPTER 4

OVERCOME ANXIETY-FILLED BEHAVIORS BY MANAGING YOUR FIXER

Discover, Experience, and Apply

Discover how your fixer drives your anxiety-filled behaviors.

Experience how defusing the fixer helps you overcome anxiety-filled behaviors.

Apply your anxiety reduction tools in your daily life.

Mind-Body Language

Fixer: The depressor's partner that drives your anxiety-filled behaviors with overactive, never-ending thoughts of how to fix yourself and the world.

Defusing the fixer: When you become clearly aware (at the time you are doing something) that your fixer is active and use your anxiety reduction tools, you take away the fixer's power. Right away, you feel a shift from a stressful, anxiety-filled state to one with a ready and relaxed mind and body. You can now calmly take care of yourself and whatever you have to do in the executive mode.

Depressor/fixer cycle: These I-System partners create a vicious cycle, keeping the I-System going and causing your anxiety symptoms.

THE HIDDEN ENEMY WITHIN: THE FIXER

Requirements, the depressor, and the fixer are the three major parts of the I-System. Requirements are the I-System's rules about how you and the world should be. When a requirement is broken, this switches on the I-System. Then the depressor and fixer jump in, interact with each other, and keep the I-System going. In this chapter we focus on the fixer. The fixer is the depressor's lifelong, faithful partner that overacts and drives you to repair the negative, painful state the depressor has caused. The fixer starts from the false belief (caused by the depressor) that you are broken, tries to fix you, and works by making you believe it's really helping you. Your fixer pressures you into feeling the urgent need to take action, such as avoiding situations, organizing excessively, washing, checking and rechecking, or collecting. When the fixer is active, enough will never be enough. You can recognize it when you notice increased body tension and a mind full of anxious thoughts like *I have to do this or something bad will happen, If I do that I'll have a heart attack,* or *I can't go shopping without my partner.* No matter what you do, the depressor will jump in with thoughts like *I can't cope* and *I'm useless,* pushing your fixer to even do more. The depressor and fixer work with each other in a depressor/fixer cycle. This cycle keeps the I-System active, and is responsible for all the various symptoms of anxiety disorders such as panic attacks, agoraphobia, phobia, obsessive-compulsive disorder (OCD), post-traumatic stress disorder (PTSD), stress disorder, and generalized anxiety disorder.

Hali, a well-respected assistant manager at a supermarket, suffered from excess worry, stomach pain, backaches, and trouble sleeping, and she often called in sick. When her manager brought her customer complaints and problems, she would immediately feel anxious and have thoughts like *It's my fault, I can't get it right,* and *I'll lose my job.* Her thoughts would spin into storylines and embed negativity into her body, making her feel weak and helpless. She would then try to cover her sense of helplessness by putting on her "calm face." When her boss left, she would work as hard as she could to address the problems. Even though her actions satisfied her boss, Hali's efforts always fell short of her own expectations. This caused her negative thoughts to race and her body to become even more distressed (ulcer, insomnia, and chronic back pain). No matter how hard she tried or how well she did, her inner anxiety and physical symptoms never went away. Her primary care doctor referred her to mind-body bridging.

Using the anxiety reduction tools of mind-body bridging, Hali began noticing her body tension and mental pressure as a sign that her I-System's fixer was active. She hadn't realized that her fixer had been in the driver's seat trying to fix the inner distress her depressor caused and that no matter how hard she tried, her fixer would never fix her inner sense of helplessness (the powerless self). In fact, her attempt at "fixing" by pushing herself more and more was giving rise to her symptoms. Most importantly, she found that for every fixer thought (for example, *Be stronger, Work harder,* or *Do more*), there was an embedded depressor thought (for example, *I'm weak* or *I can't do it*). Even when she had been successful, she had never found peace of mind or a sense of well-being. During her daily activities, whenever her stomach or back tightened, she realized it was the telltale sign of her fixer activity. Hali would then use her anxiety reduction tools before her mind-body could get into an overreactive state. Using her mind-body bridging tools in her everyday life, she drove herself less, accomplished more, and was able to sleep all night. Her anxiety-related symptoms began decreasing. Hali was learning to have her powerful self, functioning in the executive mode, in charge.

DISCOVER HOW YOUR FIXER CAUSES YOUR ANXIETY-FILLED BEHAVIOR

1. To overcome your anxiety-filled behaviors, it's critical to recognize when the fixer is in control. The following fixer map is really going to surprise you. Jot down around the oval the thoughts that come up about "How I Am Going to Improve My Life." Work quickly for a couple of minutes, without editing your thoughts.

> HOW I AM GOING TO IMPROVE MY LIFE MAP

HOW I AM GOING TO
IMPROVE MY LIFE

A. Looking at your overall map, how do you feel?

Calm _____ Tense _____ Overwhelmed _____

B. Consider each item on your map and figure out how much body tension you have when you think about going for this self-improvement goal. Next to each item on your map, note your level of body tension using one of these symbols: Ø for no body tension, + for mild, ++ for moderate, or +++ for severe. It may help to see the sample map at the end of the exercise.

The statements on your map may be either fixer thoughts from an active I-System or natural thoughts from executive functioning. The thoughts that come with body tension are fixer thoughts from your I-System, and the thoughts with no body tension are from executive functioning. Your challenge is telling the difference between the two. Body tension that comes with thoughts means your I-System is active. The fixer brings a mental urgency, creating extra pressure for you to act. Remember, executive functioning is how you think, feel, see the world, and act when your I-System is quiet. When you are in executive functioning mode and don't reach a goal, you're naturally disappointed. But when you don't reach a fixer goal, you feel devastated; your mind spins with anxious thoughts, and your body is tense. For all your efforts and good intentions to succeed, it's important to know which of your daily activities the fixer is capturing.

C. Again, look over each item on your map and imagine that you're not going to reach that goal. Describe what happens to your body tension. Note how you feel driven to act:

_____

_____

D. If you now feel body tension and mind clutter for items that were previously at level Ø, those items have become fixer thoughts. List your fixer thoughts from this map:

_____

_____

_____

E. List your thoughts on this map that are from executive functioning (tension-free):

_____

_____

2. It's important to compare the Depressor map in chapter 3 (the first map in that chapter) to this Fixer map titled "How I Am Going to Improve My Life":

A. Which map has the higher overall energy levels (makes you feel better)?

Depressor map _____   Fixer map _____

The higher levels of energy that may come with the fixer and make you believe that you feel better aren't unusual. This higher endorphin level can keep you from recognizing your fixer, because you feel good about the thoughts. When active, the fixer clouds your judgment and affects your actions. Thoughts on this map, when driven by the fixer (*Get rid of my anxiety, Be a better parent*), cause your anxiety-filled behaviors.

B. Your body is always giving you helpful information. Note the differences in location, quality, and intensity of the body tension that comes with the thoughts on the Depressor and Fixer maps (for example, *My body tension on the Depressor map was located around my gut, and my body felt heavy and unresponsive; on my Fixer map, my body tension is around my chest and head, and there's a jittery feeling*).

_____

_____

The intensity of your body tension and the driving pressure of your storylines are important signs that your I-System's fixer is active. Storylines are a sign that your fixer is restricting your ability to deal with your current situation.

SAMPLE MAP: HOW I AM GOING TO IMPROVE MY LIFE

Go to the movies +++

Be more in control +++

*Stop spending hours
reorganizing my things ++*

*Be able to do my job
without worrying about
bad things happening +++*

Have more free time +++

HOW I AM GOING TO
IMPROVE MY LIFE

Be a better parent ++

*Stop trying to second-guess
decisions +++*

Get rid of my anxiety +++

Plant flowers Ø

Fixer thoughts come with body tension when you think about trying to reach your goals or imagine that you won't reach your goals (for example, *Be a better parent, Stop spending hours reorganizing my things, Get rid of my anxiety, Go to the movies, Have more free time*). Also note any thoughts from natural functioning (without body tension, marked Ø) (for example, *Plant flowers*).

THE MASKS OF THE FIXER

The mask of the fixer takes many forms. For instance, Lou is driven to wash his hands seventy to eighty times a day. Tara is forced to rearrange her room every day. Sherri has a house full of things that she hoards and has little living space. Bob is so superstitious that his rituals take up hours per day. Kim avoids so many activities and places that her life is very limited.

The fixer activates mental pressure, stirs up your body, and urges you to act. It drives your actions and leaves you feeling anxious and helpless. Be aware of the way your fixer frames the demand. The fixer traps you into thinking, *I need to, I have to, I must*, or *I will*. When your I-System is switched on and the fixer is in the driver's seat, it can drive activities that are difficult to control (repetitive actions and avoidances), and prevent you from taking care of yourself and your responsibilities. The fixer pushes you to do things that are apparently aimed at relieving your anxiety but end up further limiting your life. Whenever your fixer is active, it drives your anxiety-filled behaviors and prevents self-healing. Notice the early signs of body tension, storylines, and mental pressure.

The fixer will mask itself as the great savior in your life. At first the fixer may seem to reduce anxiety and improve your life. Remember, the fixer's real job is to fix how the depressor makes you feel and to keep the I-System going. This supports the powerless self. At times, the fixer uses thoughts like *I'll feel better if I don't walk alone, Wash your hands to be clean, Keep checking the stove to be safe, Organize your things into their proper place*, or *Have better sex*, which hide the underlying depressor thoughts: *I'm afraid to walk alone, I'm dirty, I can't trust myself, I'm disorganized*, or *I'm not having good sex*. These hidden depressor thoughts make you feel so awful that your fixer drives your anxiety-filled activities.

Never underestimate the urgency the fixer creates when it tries to fix the powerless self. Since these fixer thoughts come with mental and physical pressure, they drive fixer activities in a failed attempt to fix how your depressor makes you feel. However, after you do the fixer-driven activity, your depressor creates more negative feelings, and this pushes the fixer back into action. This creates a stressful yo-yo effect (depressor/fixer/depressor/fixer…). All of this builds so much tension and mental turmoil that it hinders your ability to manage your anxiety and take care of your responsibilities. The fixer can also disguise itself as a helper by pushing you to stop getting anxious and limit your anxiety-filled behavior. Even when these attempts seem positive, your success doesn't often last very long because they are driven by your I-System. To break this cycle, become actively aware of the fixer's mental and physical pressure that drives your activity, and recognize your depressor, which lies beneath the surface.

YOUR FIXER HAS AN UNDERLYING DEPRESSOR

1. Every fixer has an embedded depressor that drives it. Look again at the fixer map, "How I Am Going to Improve My Life." Write down your embedded depressor thoughts under the fixer thoughts. See the following sample map.

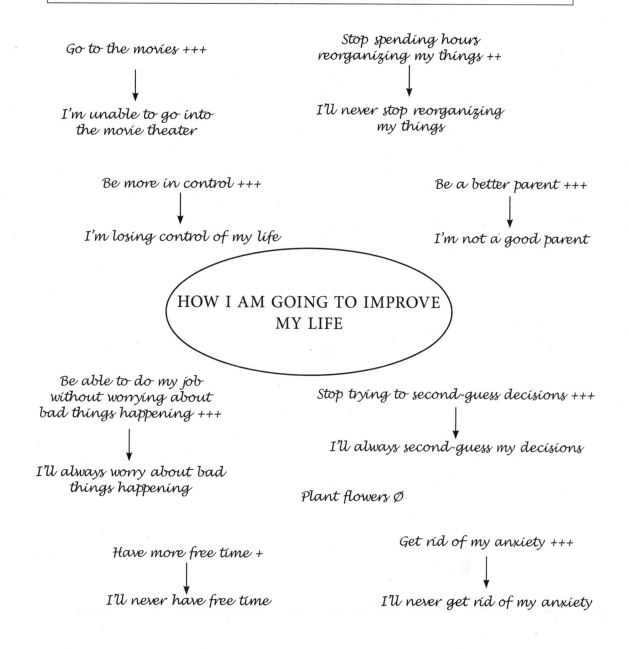

SAMPLE MAP: HOW I AM GOING TO IMPROVE MY LIFE
WITH DEPRESSOR THOUGHTS

Go to the movies +++

↓

I'm unable to go into
the movie theater

Stop spending hours
reorganizing my things ++

↓

I'll never stop reorganizing
my things

Be more in control +++

↓

I'm losing control of my life

Be a better parent +++

↓

I'm not a good parent

HOW I AM GOING TO IMPROVE
MY LIFE

Be able to do my job
without worrying about
bad things happening +++

↓

I'll always worry about bad
things happening

Stop trying to second-guess decisions +++

↓

I'll always second-guess my decisions

Plant flowers Ø

Have more free time +

↓

I'll never have free time

Get rid of my anxiety +++

↓

I'll never get rid of my anxiety

2. Think about last weekend. The fixer is always active when you attempt to escape from how the depressor makes you feel. Below, note any of your activities that created mental or physical pressure (fixer activity). Can you find the embedded depressor activity? Note your body tension with Ø for none, + for mild, ++ for moderate, or +++ for severe.

Fixer-Driven Behavior	Tension Level	Depressor Thoughts	Storyline
Washed my hands seventy-eight times.	+++	I do bad things.	I'm a bad son because I didn't call Mother. She needed me.
Kept counting my steps in the kitchen.	+++	I'm unsafe.	Counting steps makes me feel safe.
Save everything.	+++	I'll have nothing.	Saving things relieves my anxiety about the future.
Spent the weekend sharpening and cleaning tools.	+++	The tools are not right.	Tools have to be perfect, so I have to find every dull, dirty edge.
Couldn't go shopping without my friend Julie.	+++	I can't be alone with all those people.	I'll have a panic attack and be helpless without Julie.
Rearranged my living room.	+++	I can't get it right.	I need to be sure the furniture is in the right place.

A. When your fixer was active, what were the outcomes of your behavior? For example, *Rearranged my living room*: *spent hours doing it, couldn't get it right, broke a lamp.*

_____

_____

_____

_____

_____

B. When you had depressor thoughts, how did you feel?

_____

_____

C. Did your fixer jump in to fix the depressor thoughts?　Yes _____　No _____

D. How did your storylines keep the depressor/fixer cycle going?

_____

_____

_____

_____

E. What were the underlying requirements you were trying to meet?

_____

_____

_____

_____

To stop the fixer/depressor cycle and reduce the anxiety in your life, defuse the depressor and find the requirement that lies beneath the surface. With a quiet I-System, your powerful self will be in charge of your work, relationships, and play.

THE DANCE OF THE DEPRESSOR/FIXER

Not only does the depressor/fixer cycle cause sleepless nights and anxiety-filled days, it harms your relationships and prevents you from making good decisions. When you see that your depressor/fixer cycle is in action, you reduce anxiety and self-heal.

Sally, a successful twenty-five-year-old clothing designer, had a sudden and unexpected panic attack while getting ready for work. "My heart was beating so fast, I was afraid I was going to die." After ten minutes, her sweating, shortness of breath, and chest discomfort went away. Even though she was still worried about what happened, she went to work. Two weeks later Sally had another panic attack. This prompted her to go to the doctor and have a complete medical workup. After extensive testing, she received a report that her heart was normal and there was no obvious physical cause for any of her symptoms. Sally felt relieved, but she kept having more panic attacks. These ongoing attacks finally led her into mind-body bridging therapy. Developing a strong bridging awareness practice, she observed that at the beginning of her panic attacks her heart began beating harder and faster. Whenever she felt these early signs, she would immediately begin to use her bridging awareness practices and thought labeling to help calm down. This prevented some of the panic attacks. Another breakthrough came when she did a Panic Attack map. Her map had depressor items like *I'm afraid I'm going to die, I'll never make it, I'm helpless,* and *I'm trapped.* Her fixer items were *Prepare for an emergency, Regain control,* and *Try harder.* She saw her requirements, *I shouldn't have heart problems* and *I shouldn't be sick.* Sally started to sob and said that when she was in high school, her mother died of a massive heart attack. Sally then recognized that when her I-System was activated by a requirement, her depressor thoughts of dying pushed her fixer into high gear: *Prepare for an emergency, Regain control,* and *Try harder.* Remember that the fixer is there to fix the bad feelings caused by the depressor. The depressor then responds with more helplessness and fear, keeping the I-System going. Sally realized that the depressor/fixer cycle was behind her panic attacks. Two years later Sally sent a letter to her mind-body bridging therapist thanking her and saying that she was not only free of her panic attacks, but also happier and more successful than ever before.

When the I-System is active, it causes your behavior to be driven. When you avoid things or have anxiety-filled behaviors, your fixer is in the driver's seat. When you feel weak, anxious, and powerless, the depressor is in the driver's seat. The depressor and fixer have an interesting relationship. You automatically strengthen one when you push away, reject, or deny the other. For example, when you don't recognize the passive, weak, helpless thoughts the depressor has captured, the fixer becomes more energized. When you deny or fail to recognize your avoidance and anxiety-filled behaviors caused by the fixer, this results in anxious depressor thoughts and unpleasant body sensations. When the I-System is quiet, this means your depressor and fixer are no longer active, and your powerful self is in the driver's seat. Then you are anxiety-free.

WHICH TO-DOS ARE MAKING YOU ANXIOUS

We all have a list of to-dos that are part of our daily activities. The next two-part map shows you how your fixer is making it harder to get through your list without anxiety or avoidance.

1. Around the oval, jot down all the things you need to get done over the next few days that are making you anxious. Write for a couple of minutes, without editing your thoughts. The following sample map may be helpful.

TO-DO MAP

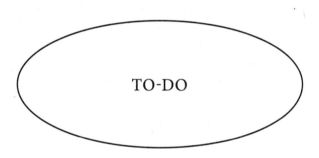

TO-DO

A. Next to each item on your map, note your level of body tension, using one of these symbols: Ø for no body tension, + for mild, ++ for moderate, or +++ for severe. It may help to see the sample map that follows. Those items with body tension are fixers.

B. List the storylines associated with the three fixers that have the most body tension:

_____

_____

_____

SAMPLE MAP: TO DO

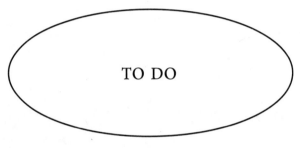

Have company over for dinner +++

Finalize plans for the new project at work +++

Pay my bills ++

Take the kids to the dentist ++

TO DO

*Go to the parent-teacher
conference* +++

*Go shopping for my son's
birthday present* +++

Get car serviced +

Call Mom +++

Exercise ++

Sample storylines:

Call Mom: *I should call her now. Nothing satisfies her. She criticizes me. She always tells me how to live my life.*

Go to the parent-teacher conference: *Charlie won't do his homework. His teacher always blames me. She talks down to me.*

Finalize plans for the new project at work: *My boss keeps changing the plan. I can't leave anything out. What if I make a mistake? This could end my career.*

2. Now do the map again, this time using your bridging awareness practices, and see what happens. Before you start writing, listen to background sounds, feel your body's pressure on your seat, sense your feet on the floor, and feel the pen in your hand. Take your time. Once you're settled, keep feeling the pen in your hand, and start writing. Scatter your thoughts around the oval. Watch the ink go onto the paper, and listen to background sounds. Write for a couple of minutes.

TO-DO MAP WITH BRIDGING

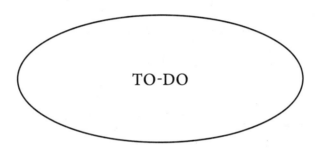

A. Compare the two maps. What do you notice?

_____

B. In this mind-body state, how do you experience your to-do list?

_____

_____

The release of body tension, and the reduced mind clutter and sense of urgency, mean that you have shifted into executive functioning. You learned that it was the depressor/fixer cycle, with its related storylines, that made you feel overwhelmed and anxious, not what you have to do. Without the I-System adding anxiety and taking away your self-power, you manage the things you have to do much better and more naturally.

Now that you have calmed your I-System, it's time for you to take care of your to-do list with your powerful self in charge.

UNMASKING YOUR FIXER

Your days are filled with activities. Many of them may be free of anxiety (for example, playing with your dog or watching your favorite TV show). Others (for example, rushing to an appointment or meeting, pushing yourself to meet a deadline, dealing with a never-ending list of demands for your time) could well come with body tension and storylines (anxious and worried self-talk). When you unmask the fixer, your activities that were filled with tension are now tension-free and are carried out with a quiet I-System.

Think back over the last twenty-four hours and notice the specific body tension, mental pressure, or feelings of being driven. That's your fixer in action. See the different characteristics of body tension (location, type, or both) that come with your fixer. Noticing the early signs of fixer body tension is the key to preventing a full-blown anxiety attack.

Activity	Body Tension and Location	Storyline	Fixer-Driven Thought
Straighten up the garage.	*Tense neck, chest pressure*	*It's so disorganized, I'll never get it finished.*	*If I really work at it, I'll get it perfect.*

The fixer may also be involved when you can't seem to move on from an issue. Maybe at night, when you're trying to sleep, thoughts about whether you did or didn't do something play over and over in your mind. Your I-System's fixer is in high gear, interfering with your sleep as you try to figure the situation out or plan to fix it. Doing a two-part What's on My Mind map before bed is very helpful. Remember to also use bridging awareness practices and thought labeling to get a good night's sleep. Quality sleep is your number one way to revitalize, whereas poor sleep can cause you to start the next day tired and anxious.

SITUATIONS YOU WANT TO AVOID

1. Think about a situation that you want to avoid (*Getting into an elevator* or *Flying*). Write it in the oval. For several minutes, jot down around the oval any thoughts that come up about that situation. The following sample map may be helpful.

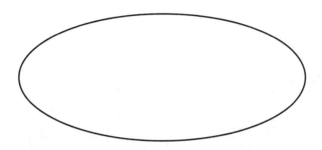

WHAT I DON'T LIKE TO DO MOST MAP

A. Describe your initial body tension and how it progresses to anxiety:

_____

_____

B. List your depressors and storylines:

_____

_____

C. List your requirements:

_____

_____

D. In this mind-body state, how do you feel and act?

_____

SAMPLE MAP: WHAT I DON'T LIKE TO DO MOST

I won't ride in an elevator.

Elevators get stuck all the time.

I'd walk up twenty flights of stairs before I'll use the elevator.

All those people packed in like sardines.

I'll be helpless there.

GETTING INTO AN ELEVATOR

I'm sweating just thinking about it.

The last time I did it, I nearly died from my heart racing and had trouble breathing.

I couldn't do it even if the elevator was empty.

A. Describe your initial body tension and how it progresses to anxiety: *Tight chest progressing to shortness of breath and racing heart.*

B. List your depressors and storylines: *Helpless; I'll never get over my fear.*

C. List your requirements: *I shouldn't ride in an elevator.*

D. In this mind-body state, how do you feel and act? *Terrified, and avoid elevators.*

2. You just experienced how your I-System works. It makes you anxious and prevents you from doing things. Let's do the map again, this time using your bridging awareness practices, and see what happens. Write the same goal in the oval. Before you start writing, listen to background sounds, feel your body's pressure on your seat, sense your feet on the floor, and feel the pen in your hand. Take your time. Once you're settled, keep feeling the pen in your hand, and start writing. Scatter your thoughts around the oval. Watch the ink go onto the paper, and listen to background sounds. Write for a couple of minutes.

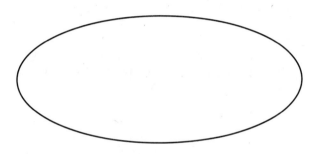

WHAT I WANT TO AVOID MAP WITH BRIDGING

Look at the items on your map. The thoughts that come without excess body tension, anxiety, and mental pressure indicate executive functioning and the presence of your powerful self. What are they?

_____

_____

_____

Both maps you just did had the same situation in the oval. In the first map, you saw how your I-System adds anxiety, mind clutter, body tension, and depressor/fixer activity. In the second map, you quieted your I-System with your bridging awareness tools and shifted into executive functioning. In this state, your powerful self is in control. When your I-System is at rest, you have the choice of doing or not doing the things you previously wanted to avoid.

DEFUSING YOUR FIXER TO OVERCOME ANXIETY-FILLED BEHAVIORS

Your day consists of one activity after another. Each activity you are doing or not doing throughout the day is either from executive functioning or driven by the fixer. Anxiety is only possible with an active fixer. The only time you can defuse and stop your fixer is in the midst of an activity. When you stop the depressor/fixer cycle and calm your I-System, your powerful self controls the activity while in the executive mode. Throughout the day, notice the activity of your fixer: body tension, mental pressure, the depressor/fixer cycle, and storylines. When your fixer is active, use these steps to defuse it:

1. As soon as you notice any body tension, mental urgency, and spinning negative or anxious storylines, know that your fixer is in action.

2. Use bridging awareness practices and thought labeling to quiet your I-System.

3. Be on the lookout for new stories that the I-System's fixer (or embedded depressor) may spin about how the fixer can help you. These storylines impair your judgment and cause more anxiety-filled behaviors.

4. When the fixer is active, find the depressor that lies beneath the surface. Know that the fixer's real motive is to relieve the pain and dysfunction caused by the depressor (powerless self). When you defuse the depressor, you automatically reduce the pressure and urgency of the fixer and shift into your powerful self.

5. Remember, it's not the activity you are doing but who's doing it that is important. If it is your I-System's powerless self, your behaviors will be filled with anxiety. If it's your powerful self, functioning in the executive mode, your activities will be anxiety-free.

You know when you have defused your fixer, because your I-System is quiet, your body is calm, and your activities are being done by your powerful self, not the pressure-driven fixer. You witness firsthand that the powerless self is a false belief. You are not broken and don't need fixing. Executive functioning is your birthright.

Tina, a stressed-out and anxious mother, had trouble telling the difference between fixer thoughts and those from natural executive functioning, until she began using her anxiety reduction tools throughout the day. She starts the day by using her morning shower as a bridging awareness practice. She feels the warmth of the water as it touches her skin, and listens to the sounds of the shower. If a pressure-driven thought comes up, she labels that thought as just a thought and continues her shower. Using these practices every day, Tina calms her mind and body. Now when she looks at the clock, thinks *The kids will be late for school. We need to hurry*, and feels her shoulders tighten, she knows that her usual response of yelling "You'll be late for school! Hurry up!" comes from her fixer. She again labels her thoughts and uses her bridging awareness practices. She listens to the traffic sounds outside the window, feels her feet as she walks across the hall, feels her shoulders drop, and calmly gathers everyone. She has defused her fixer in real time, the only place you can, and returned to executive functioning.

In the heat of any situation, you, too, can convert the fixer into natural executive functioning. Remember, the only time to defuse and stop your fixer is *during* an activity. Use your fixer recognition tools for several days and then fill out the chart below.

Activity	Telltale Signs of Your Fixer	Anxiety Reduction Tools You Used	Results
Getting the kids ready for school.	*Breathing faster, shoulders pulled up, do-or-die sense of urgency*	*Listened to background sounds. Stayed aware of my body.*	*Calmly got kids ready for school.*
Excessive hand washing.	*Urgency to wash hands*	*Recognized my fixer in action. Did map and noticed depressor thought, "I didn't help my brother when he called this morning."*	*Felt less urgency to wash my hands.*
Avoiding going to college social event.	*Avoidance of something I wanted to do*	*Noticed underlying depressor, "I'm awkward and unattractive." Did two-part map.*	*Felt less anxious and went to event. Had a good time.*

We are so used to our fixer pushing us that we have come to accept what it does with an *It's just me* attitude. How many times have you felt anxious, driven, or inhibited, and dismissed it as *It's just me*? Remember, when your I-System is on, you can defuse your fixer by simply being aware that it is active. Doing a two-part map is very helpful. Then use your bridging awareness tools to bring your awareness back to what you were doing. The tough part is noticing the early signs of your active depressor and fixer. To do this, it helps to have a strong daily bridging awareness practice. Then as soon as you start to have body tension, negative storylines, mental pressure, and feelings of being pushed, you know it's the fixer. Using all your anxiety reduction tools gradually overcomes your anxiety symptoms.

YOU ARE NOT BROKEN AND DON'T NEED FIXING

As you have seen on the How I Am Going to Improve My Life map, the fixer tries to present itself as a valued helper. Many people believe that their success in life is due to the drive and pressure of the fixer, and even say, "If it weren't for all this tension, I would never have accomplished anything."

1. Do a map titled "What Will Happen if I Give Up My Fixer." Jot down whatever comes to mind when you imagine giving up your fixer (for example, *I'll be taken advantage of*, *I'll lose my job*, *I'll never accomplish anything*, or *I'll be a wreck*). Write for a couple of minutes. Describe your body tension at the bottom of the map.

WHAT WILL HAPPEN IF I GIVE UP MY FIXER MAP

WHAT WILL HAPPEN IF
I GIVE UP MY FIXER?

Body Tension: _____

A. Look at your map and list some of your requirements:

_____

_____

_____

B. In this mind-body state, how do you act?

_____

Some people become anxious when they do this map. They have come to rely on the fixer to face and control situations that make them uncomfortable. They feel as if they'll lose who they are and become weak if they give up their fixers. People think, *To give up my fixer would be like giving up my right arm!* and *If I let my fixer go, I'll go right down the tubes.* They fear that if they relax, they will be powerless and fail. This reliance on the fixer's power is the I-System's false promise that can never be fulfilled because enough will never be enough. The next map will demonstrate that when you quiet your I-System, you free yourself from the tyranny of your fixer and experience your self-healing powers.

2. Do the previous map again, this time using your bridging awareness practices. Before you start writing, listen to background sounds, feel your body's pressure on your seat, sense your feet on the floor, and feel the pen in your hand. Take your time. Once you're settled, keep feeling the pen in your hand, and start writing. Watch the ink go onto the paper, and listen to background sounds. Write for a couple of minutes.

WHAT WILL HAPPEN IF I GIVE UP MY FIXER MAP WITH BRIDGING

WHAT WILL HAPPEN IF I GIVE
UP MY FIXER?

A. List two fixer-driven behaviors that have caused difficulties in your life:

_____

_____

B. Are you ready to let go of them?   Yes _____   No _____

C. When you are in executive-functioning mode instead of in the spin of the I-System, do you feel that you are not broken and don't need fixing?   Yes _____   No _____

With a resting I-System, your powerful self is in the driver's seat. In this unified mind-body state, you have access your wellspring of healing, goodness, and wisdom, which gives you the strength and energy to take care of yourself and everything you have to do without anxiety.

WHO IS DOING IT?

"What should I do?" and "How should I handle my anxiety?" are frequently asked questions. But they aren't the right questions. The real issue is not *what* you should do or *how* you should do it, but *who* is doing it: your powerless self (active I-System) or the powerful self in the executive mode. If your I-System is overactive and your powerless self is in charge, then you will have anxious thoughts and anxiety-filled behaviors. When your I-System is quiet, your powerful self, functioning in the executive mode, is in the driver's seat, calmly taking the best action to deal with any situation as it arises.

During the day, ask yourself who is doing the activity (walking, parenting, using the computer, paying bills, working, getting frustrated, playing, and so forth). Is it your anxiety-filled self, driven by an overactive I-System, or is it your natural powerful self? Remember, it's not the activity but who's doing it that matters. Awareness of who's doing an activity helps you shift from the powerless self to the powerful self. Try it and describe what happened:

_____

_____

_____

_____

_____

_____

DON'T LET YOUR FIXER FOOL YOU

The I-System is not a static system; it may try to fool you by creating more fixers. For your continued progress, it's important to recognize new fixers as they come up. Some examples are:

I'm doing better, so I can relax and not do as much bridging.

I'm good enough that I can do the maps in my head.

It's okay to be anxious once in a while if the situation calls for it.

I only need to bridge when I'm tense or anxious.

Avoiding things is okay.

Natural executive functioning is always effortless, so I don't need to practice anymore.

These fixers parade themselves as choices that come from natural executive functioning. But they have the same distinct signs you learned earlier in this chapter (body tension, mental pressure, urgent storylines, and not seeing the effects of your actions). What is new is that they offer themselves in a way that makes you feel good about them and you fail to notice the higher level of tension that is driving the choice. The fixer takes the path of least resistance. When you recognize the fixer and reduce your tension with your bridging awareness practices, your powerful self makes the choice, free of the influence of the I-System.

APPLY YOUR ANXIETY REDUCTION TOOLS IN YOUR DAILY LIFE

Remember, all your actions throughout the day are either from natural executive functioning or driven by the fixer. The fixer drives all of the different shapes and forms of anxiety. Recall that once a requirement (rule) is broken, the I-System is active. The depressor then grabs negative thoughts, spinning them into storylines that lead to an unpleasant mind-body state. Next the fixer jumps in to try to repair this negative state. These fixer activities lead to a mind-body state filled with anxiety. When you recognize your I-System at work and then use your anxiety reduction tools, your powerful self is back in the driver's seat.

Madge, with an excellent driving record, was involved in a bad car accident that was not her fault. She developed a lot of anxiety about driving, and just thinking about getting behind the wheel of her car filled her mind with memories of the accident and made her heart race. Madge discovered mind-body bridging. She learned about her depressor/fixer cycle, how it created her fears, and how this I-System activity was the cause of her anxiety. Her fixer would pressure her to get over the accident and start driving again immediately. Her depressor would come in with negative thoughts about how she could get hit again. Then her fixer jumped in with the thought, *"So don't drive."* Her storylines were all about how dangerous other drivers are and how they couldn't be trusted. When Madge mapped out her anxiety, she found her requirements were *"I should be able to handle any driving situation"* and *"People should be just as cautious when driving as I am."* She began to quiet her I-System by using bridging awareness practices and thought labeling as effective tools to "calm down." Soon Madge was ready to drive again. Now when Madge is driving and her thoughts begin to spin, she recognizes that her fixer/depressor cycle is active, labels her thoughts, feels the steering wheel, hears the sounds of the road, pays attention to the roadway, and calmly continues to drive.

Anxiety Reduction Tools

➢   Defuse the fixer.

➢   Recognize the depressor/fixer cycle.

➢   Convert fixer activity into executive functioning.

MBB RATING SCALE: OVERCOME ANXIETY-FILLED BEHAVIORS BY MANAGING YOUR FIXER

Date: _____

After using the tools in this chapter for several days, check the description that most closely reflects your practice: hardly ever, sometimes, usually, or almost always.

How often do you...	Hardly Ever	Sometimes	Usually	Almost Always
Notice the fixer's never-ending pressure and tension?				
Become aware of the body sensations associated with the fixer?				
Realize that the fixer can never fix the powerless self?				
Find the depressor embedded in the fixer?				
Notice when the depressor/fixer cycle is active?				
Recognize the storylines that come with the fixer?				
Reduce your anxiety by recognizing your fixer?				
Notice the difference between fixer-driven activities and activities from natural executive functioning?				
Realize that the fixer is not necessary for your success?				
Notice a reduction of anxiety when you defuse your fixer in real time?				

List the main body sensations you have when the fixer is in control:

_____

List anxious thoughts or behaviors the fixer causes:

_____

How did your anxiety change when you recognized your fixer and shifted into executive functioning?

_____

_____

MBB QUALITY OF LIFE GAUGE

Date: _____

Only do this indicator when you have made a habit in your life of using the anxiety reduction tools from the first four chapters. It lets you measure your progress and keep track of your life-changing experiences.

Over the past seven days, how did you do in these areas?

Circle the number under your answer.	Not at all	Several days	More than half the days	Nearly every day
1. I've had positive interest and pleasure in my activities.	0	1	3	5
2. I've felt optimistic, excited, and hopeful.	0	1	3	5
3. I've slept well and woken up feeling refreshed.	0	1	3	5
4. I've had lots of energy.	0	1	3	5
5. I've been able to focus on tasks and use self-discipline.	0	1	3	5
6. I've stayed healthy, eaten well, exercised, and had fun.	0	1	3	5
7. I've felt good about my relationships with my family and friends.	0	1	3	5
8. I've been satisfied with my accomplishments at home, work, or school.	0	1	3	5
9. I've been comfortable with my financial situation.	0	1	3	5
10. I've felt good about the spiritual base of my life.	0	1	3	5
11. I've been satisfied with the direction of my life.	0	1	3	5
12. I've felt fulfilled, with a sense of well-being and peace of mind.	0	1	3	5

Score Key: Column Total ____ ____ ____ ____

0–15 .... Poor

16–30 .... Fair   Total Score _____

31–45 .... Good

46 and above .... Excellent

CHAPTER 5

DEFUSE YOUR REQUIREMENTS TO PREVENT ANXIETY

Discover, Experience, and Apply

Discover how requirements are the root cause of anxiety.

Experience how defusing your requirements prevents anxiety.

Apply the anxiety reduction tools in your daily life.

Mind-Body Language

Defusing requirements: When you use all your anxiety reduction tools, you handle a situation that used to make you anxious (turn on your I-System) with a ready and relaxed mind-body free of anxiety. Even when the I-System's picture of how you and the world should be is not fulfilled, the requirement is powerless to turn on your I-System and cause anxiety.

YOUR OFF/ON ANXIETY SWITCH

The I-System, like a light switch, is either off or on. The natural state of the I-System is off. When it's off, you are in the executive mode with your mind and body in harmony and balance. Your ability to respond to situations is at its best. This is your powerful self.

This harmony and balance is only disrupted when the I-System is turned on by a requirement. Once active, the depressor and fixer keep the I-System going. The depressor acts by slowing down or even paralyzing your mind and body functions (perceiving, thinking, feeling, and acting). Your mind is filled with troubling thoughts and your body is heavy and lethargic. The fixer acts by excessively speeding up your mind and body. Your mind spins with anxious, pressure-driven thoughts, and your body is tense. Because you are so anxious and overstimulated, responding in a healthy way to situations is difficult. When you recognize and defuse your requirements you control the off/on switch.

Mia, a married, successful physician, had a fear of snakes since childhood, when neighborhood boys would chase and tease the girls with snakes. Mia went through college, medical school, and residency without giving any thought to her fear. She and her family settled down in a small midwestern town where every summer there would be snakes in her yard. Although they were nonpoisonous, whenever she saw a snake, Mia would become petrified, break out into a sweat, and have a rapid heartbeat. This would be followed by fifteen minutes of misery and vomiting. It would take her a half hour to settle down. Mia couldn't understand her snake phobia because she was comfortable with spiders, insects, lizards, and other creatures. Nothing in her medical practice had created any anxiety. She loved working in her yard and garden before snake season. To the amusement of her friends, once the snakes showed up for the summer, she wouldn't set foot in anyone's yard. Mia wanted to get past this phobia and tried many things including snake deterrents (that didn't work well enough). She even tried to desensitize herself by going to the snake house at the zoo. Although the snakes were behind glass, and she stood as far away as possible, she raced out and vomited.

Her neighbor suggested mind-body bridging. Mia built a strong foundation of bridging awareness practices and thought labeling that let her switch off her I-System. She learned about her depressor/fixer cycle, and began to do daily maps. When she had integrated all of the anxiety reduction tools into her daily life, Mia did a Snake map. It was filled with depressors: *They could squeeze me to death, They have fangs that bite deep, I could die from the bite,* and *My cousin lost her leg to a snake bite.* Her fixers were: *Stay away from all snakes,* and *Don't go out in the yard until they are gone for the season.* Mia did many maps on snakes and saw how her depressor thought (*I could die*) and its accompanying body sensations (painful, almost paralyzing feeling in her stomach and heart) activated her fixer thought (*This is a life-threatening emergency*), accompanied by total body overstimulation (rapid heart rate, sweating, rapid shallow breathing) which led to panic attacks. When her I-System was switched on, she had no choice but to avoid snakes or have a panic attack. Once she realized that it was her depressor/fixer cycle causing her symptoms, and not the snakes, her maps became more settled and her body tension lessened. Mia began going into her yard and one day, while sitting on the ground working on a flower bed, she came face to face with a snake. She jumped and rather than have a panic attack or run away, Mia used her bridging awareness practices and thought labeling, switched off her I-System, and looked at the snake eye to eye. Even though she still didn't particularly like the creature, she shooed him away, and then continued her gardening. Mia had defused her requirement in real time (the only place it can be defused) and was no longer plagued with panic attacks.

Figure 5.1 shows how your mind works. All thoughts naturally flow into the lower, executive-functioning loop when your I-System is switched off. In this unified mind-body state, your powerful self is in charge, and you live your best life. This lower loop is your birthright. No matter who you are or what you have been through, you can experience and express your powerful self, right here, right now. Your powerful self is always present and is not tainted or impaired by your anxiety symptoms. This lower loop isn't something to aim for; it's always with you, and you experience it each and every time your I-System is switched off. With your powerful self in charge, you can work your way through any difficult situations that may come up. For example, when you are in the executive-functioning loop and you face a new tough situation, your powerful self has the ability to deal with your constantly changing reality. Compare this to facing a new tough situation when you are in the I-System loop. Here, your coping and problem-solving skills are limited by requirements, and the actions of the depressor/fixer cycle result in anxiety overload and impaired functioning.

All thoughts begin as executive functioning and are free of the I-System. Requirements are formed when the I-System takes hold of thoughts to form a set of rules and a picture of how you and the world should be at any moment. As long as events do not break a requirement (rule), the I-System is off and all your thoughts, feelings, perceptions, and actions are from executive functioning. But when an event breaks a requirement, the I-System becomes active, with the depressor using negative thoughts to create unpleasant body tension. The fixer, in turn, uses thoughts to try to undo or repair the negative mind-body state the depressor caused. The depressor/fixer cycle creates your anxiety and impaired functioning. To keep the depressor/fixer cycle going, the I-System creates storylines.

In this chapter, you will map requirements that you have for yourself, others, and situations. Don't let your I-System fool you into thinking you can do maps in your head. When you put your thoughts on paper and notice your body sensations, a powerful mind-body free-association process takes place. The unexpected thought is often the requirement that lies beneath the surface. This is where your "aha" moments can happen. Each mapping exercise is set up in a way that increases your insights into each situation. The more you are in the executive-functioning loop, the quicker and easier it is to recognize and defuse your requirements as they arise in your life. Recognizing a requirement means that when you start to become anxious, you are able to identify the mental rule that has been broken about how you and the world should be. Defusing a requirement means that you now face a situation that used to cause anxiety and meltdowns with a ready, relaxed mind and body. No matter what the situation is, defusing requirements keeps your I-System turned off. Making a habit of using your anxiety reduction tools means you will live more and more of your life in the anxiety-free executive-functioning loop.

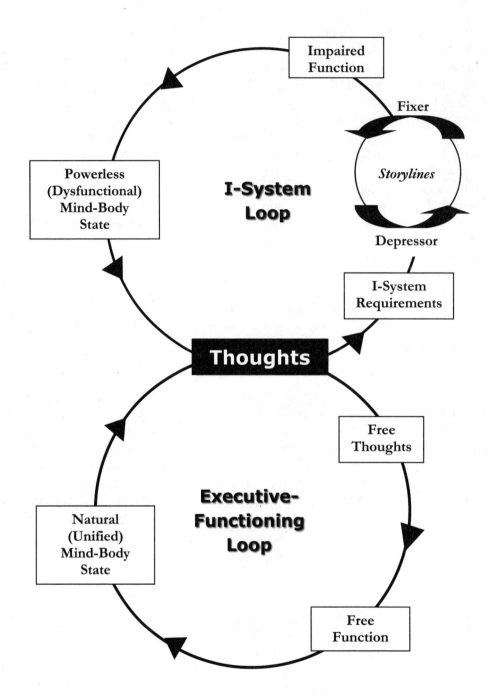

Figure 5.1 The I-System loop and the executive-functioning loop.

The mind works with thoughts. They flow in a natural way into the executive-functioning loop, where you take care of yourself and your responsibilities without anxiety. Free thoughts and free functioning are how you think, see the world, and act with an I-System at rest. When your thoughts become requirements for you and the world, you are pulled into the I-System loop, where the mind-body commotion of the I-System creates a life that is not satisfying and is filled with anxiety.

KEEP YOUR ANXIETY SWITCH OFF IN A DISTRESSING EXPERIENCE

1. There are times when someone's inappropriate behavior creates a stressful situation. Map the most distressing recent experience resulting from the behavior of another person. Write the behavior at the top of the map (*My husband keeps calling an old girlfriend*), and write how you wanted that person to act (*My husband should not call an old girlfriend*) in the oval. Take a couple of minutes to write your thoughts around the oval as you think about that person's behavior.

DISTRESSING EXPERIENCE MAP

Other Person's Behavior: _____

A. What is your body tension and how does it progress?

_____

_____

B. Is your distress and behavior due to the other person's behavior or the requirement in the oval?

_____

C. How do you act in this mind-body state?

_____

    If you believe that your distress and behavior were a result of the other person's behavior, you are letting yourself be a victim of what has happened. As long as you do not see that how you wanted the other person to act is *your* requirement, you will suffer distress and stay in the I-System loop. When you recognize your requirement and see what it is doing to you, you start a dramatic mental and physical shift so that you are no longer a victim of other people's behavior.

2. Write the same behavior on the following line. In the oval again, write how you wanted that other person to act. Before you continue writing, listen to background sounds, feel your body's pressure on your seat, sense your feet on the floor, and feel the pen in your hand. Take your time. Once you feel settled, keep feeling the pen in your hand and start writing. Watch the ink go onto the paper and listen to background sounds. Write for a couple of minutes.

DISTRESSING EXPERIENCE MAP WITH BRIDGING

Other Person's Behavior: _____

A. How is this map the same as or different from the previous map?

_____

_____

B. How do you act in this mind-body state?

_____

C. Are you a victim of circumstance?   Yes _____   No _____

D. Is the anxiety switch in your I-System turned off?   Yes _____   No _____

On the first map in this exercise, the statement in the oval was a requirement, because it switched on your I-System. After using your bridging awareness tools to quiet your I-System, that same statement was *no longer* a requirement. It became a natural thought or expectation, because your I-System was calm and your body tension and mind clutter were greatly reduced. You are now ready to deal with that same situation with a clear mind and relaxed body. Your mind-body bridging practice doesn't take away your natural expectations of how others should behave, but it does remove the distress and anxiety that your requirements cause.

FINDING REQUIREMENTS THAT CAUSE YOUR DISTRESS

Laurie had a traumatic childhood, a violent marriage (which she left), and four children who were trau-matized and acting out. She had frequent bouts of anxiety and tried to cope by compulsively cleaning, sanitizing every surface in her home daily, and trying to control everything around her. When her anxiety was triggered, she would cry hysterically, talk loudly on and on, begin to shake, and have difficulty breath-ing. People would move away from her and tell her she was "crazy."

Referred to mind-body bridging therapy, Laurie gradually began to learn and use the anxiety reduc-tion tools in her daily life. Her bouts of anxiety became fewer, and when she did have one, she was able to calm herself by tuning into sounds, touching things, and feeling her feet on the floor. She grew skilled at recognizing her requirements and defusing them in real time. She reported that when she forgot to recognize her requirement, she would have anxiety symptoms, but they were less severe. Shortly after having an episode, she would notice that her I-System was activated, recognize the requirement, and become calm. Her behavior became settled and appropriate to the situation. As she grew less anxious and compulsive, she began to feel that she was able to handle the difficult challenges of her life and gain the respect of others. More importantly, she felt respect for herself. Now, Laurie has the ability to deal with life with her powerful self in charge.

List the situations from the past few days that prompted you to become upset, tense, anxious, or overwhelmed. Realize that it's always the underlying requirement that you weren't yet aware of, and not the event, that's causing your distress. Recognizing your underlying requirement prompts changes in your thoughts and actions.

Situation	How You Handled the Situation	Unfulfilled Requirement
My spouse said I'll never change.	*I started shaking and cried.*	*My spouse should accept that I have problems.*
The owner of the company visited our office and asked to speak to me.	*I was so nervous my sweaty hands shook and I could barely speak.*	*I should be calm, cool, and collected when meeting the company owner.*

LOOK BACK AT A VERY ANXIETY-FILLED DAY

1. Think about the most anxiety-filled day you've had in the last several weeks. Jot down whatever comes to mind when you think about that day. Write for a couple of minutes. Describe your body tension at the bottom of the map.

> ## ANXIETY-FILLED DAY MAP

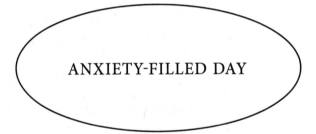

A. Describe your body tension and its progression:

_____

B. List your depressor and fixer thoughts:

_____

C. List the requirements you had for yourself:

_____

_____

D. How did you feel and act in this mind-body state?

_____

2. Now do a bridging map about that same anxiety-filled day. Before you start writing, listen to any background sounds, feel your body's pressure on your seat, sense your feet on the floor, and feel the pen in your hand. Take your time. Once you feel settled, keep feeling the pen in your hand, and start writing. Watch the ink go onto the paper, and listen to any background sounds. For the next few minutes, jot down whatever thoughts pop into your mind.

ANXIETY-FILLED DAY MAP WITH BRIDGING

ANXIETY-FILLED DAY

A. Is your body tense or relaxed?

_____

B. How do you feel and act in this mind-body state?

_____

C. Are you beginning to understand that your I-System, and not the difficulties in your day, causes you distress?   Yes _____   No _____

D. Go back and defuse the requirements on the previous map. How did it go?

_____

When you use your anxiety reduction tools every day, they will help you reduce your anxiety about situations that come up in your life.

HANDLE DISTRESSING ANXIETY WITH YOUR ANXIETY SWITCH OFF

1. Do a Distressing Anxiety Symptom map. Pick an anxiety symptom that has been causing you trouble, and write that symptom in the oval. Take a couple of minutes to jot whatever thoughts come to mind.

DISTRESSING ANXIETY SYMPTOM MAP

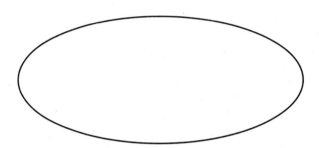

A. Describe your body tension and its progression:

_____

B. How do you feel and act in this mind-body state?

_____

C. Identify the requirements on your map:

_____

_____

_____

_____

The commotion of your I-System has you feeling distressed, anxious, and hopeless, and believing that anyone in your shoes would feel the same way. Now ask yourself, *Isn't it bad enough that I feel anxious? Why do I have to let my I-System cause a meltdown, limiting my ability to deal with and heal my anxiety?* Remember, you have no control of what life throws your way. You do have control over whether you defuse your requirements, reduce your anxiety symptoms, and heal your anxiety disorder.

2. Do this map using your bridging awareness practices. Write that same distressing anxiety symptom in the oval. Before you continue writing, listen to any background sounds, feel your body's pressure on your seat, sense your feet on the floor, and feel the pen in your hand. Take your time. Once you feel settled, keep feeling the pen in your hand, and start writing. Watch the ink go onto the paper, and listen to any background sounds. For the next few minutes, jot down whatever thoughts pop into your mind.

DISTRESSING ANXIETY SYMPTOM MAP WITH BRIDGING

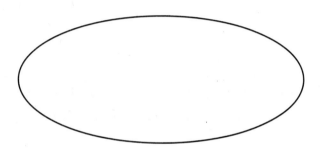

A. What is the difference in mind-body states between the two maps?

_____

_____

B. Can you see that it's your active I-System, not the anxiety symptom, that's causing your distress? Yes _____ No _____

C. In real time, which anxiety reduction tools will you use to stay in the executive mode while dealing with your symptom?

_____

You now know firsthand that it's your active I-System, not you or your anxiety disorder, that causes your anxiety and misery and keeps you from experiencing your powerful self. This map also shows the power of a strong daily bridging awareness practice. When you feel body tension, use your bridging awareness tools to create the emotional space you need to defuse requirements and deal with relationship problems and tough situations during your busy day.

MY PERFECT WORLD: POSSIBLE OR IMPOSSIBLE?

Do a How My World Would Look If My Requirements Were Met map. Scatter your thoughts around the oval for a couple of minutes. Be as specific as you can (for example, *My spouse would always take care of me, My friends would be more understanding of my condition, I would not worry so much*).

> ### HOW MY WORLD WOULD LOOK IF
> ### MY REQUIREMENTS WERE MET MAP

HOW MY WORLD WOULD
LOOK IF MY REQUIREMENTS
WERE MET

Looking back over your map, what do you notice?

_____

_____

_____

_____

_____

Even if you and your partner, boss, friends, and neighbors met all your requirements, your active I-System would always create new mental rules about how you and the world should be at any moment. Defusing requirements is a skill that helps you keep the I-System quiet and keeps your powerful self in charge without anxiety.

RECOGNIZE AND DEFUSE REQUIREMENTS TO PREVENT ANXIETY

When you get distressed, overwhelmed, and anxious, that means you have a requirement that you aren't yet aware of. Use these steps to help you recognize and defuse your requirements:

1. Be aware of the first signs that your I-System is active (for example, notice specific body tension and then the depressor, fixer, and anxious storyline activity). Let these signs prompt you to look for the requirement that lies beneath the surface.

2. Practice recognizing and defusing requirements that come up in simple situations (for example, shopping in a store when there are few customers, or going for a short walk). As it becomes easier, begin to use your skills in more complex relationships and situations.

3. Use your thought labeling and bridging awareness practice tools to stop the commotion of the I-System and then find the requirement that lies beneath the surface. Remind yourself that it's *your* requirement about the activity, person, or situation—*not* the activity, person, or situation—that's causing your distress and anxiety.

4. Once you feel a release of body tension and mind clutter (whether over time or suddenly) about the situation, you have quieted your I-System and shifted into the executive mode. The turmoil that used to be out of control melts into something that you can manage better. This is proof that you have recognized your requirement for that situation. Facing that same situation again without anxiety means you have defused the requirement.

A newly married stepmother became very anxious when her and her husband's families blended and moved in together. She had anxiety symptoms of shaking, chest discomfort, pounding heart, and insomnia. These symptoms interfered with her ability to take care of her responsibilities, and created conflict with her new husband. After beginning a mind-body bridging practice, her mapping revealed the following requirements: *My stepson should like me, My stepson shouldn't move in with his biological mother (my husband would blame me)*. Using her anxiety reduction tools to defuse her requirements lessened her anxiety. She gained the ability to take care of her blended family, and resumed a positive relationship with her husband.

Describe what happened when you used your anxiety reduction tools in real time to recognize your requirements in a situation that filled you with anxiety.

_____

_____

Describe a situation when you prevented anxiety from happening by defusing a requirement.

_____

_____

When you quiet your I-System and defuse your requirements, you are in the executive-functioning loop (figure 5.1), where your powerful self is in charge.

DIFFICULT-TO-DEFUSE REQUIREMENTS

Your I-System has been very busy defining how you and your world should be. Some requirements are easy to defuse, while others haven't budged. For the requirements that are harder for you to defuse, it helps to first focus on the situation (for example, going to your wife's company party) or thought that triggered your requirement (for example, *I shouldn't have to go to the party*) and then break that situation or thought down into smaller parts. For example, break the overall requirement down into many smaller, specific requirements: *There should not be lots of people, There should be an easy-to-get-to exit, My wife should stay close, I shouldn't worry so much about meeting her coworkers, I should be social.* When you uncover this set of specific requirements associated with this situation, use your anxiety reduction tools on each of them. Remember, after you recognize a requirement, it's ready to be defused in real time.

Over the next few days, recognize and defuse your requirements as they come up.

1. Describe which anxiety reduction tools worked best for you:

_____

2. List the requirements you were able to defuse and those you were *not* able to defuse:

Was Able to Defuse	Could Not Defuse
I shouldn't shop in a busy store. *I shouldn't spend so much time worrying.*	*I shouldn't have to fly.* *My son should do his homework.*

In dealing with a requirement like *My son should do his homework*, your I-System would have you believe that you are a bad parent because he doesn't do his homework. Remember, the goal of mind-body bridging is not to get your son to do his homework, but to defuse your requirement that he should do his homework. By doing so, you shift into executive mode and can use your natural wisdom to relate to your son in a different way. Figure 1.1 illustrates how your ability to do this expands.

3. From the previous chart, choose the requirement that has been the most difficult to defuse (for example, *I shouldn't have to fly*). Write it in the oval. Next, write your thoughts around the oval for a couple of minutes without editing them. Describe your body tension at the bottom of the map.

> ## MOST DIFFICULT TO DEFUSE REQUIREMENT MAP

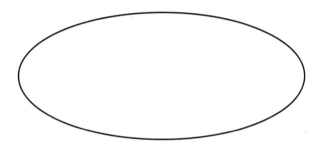

A. What is your body tension and how does it progress?

_____

B. What are your depressors?

_____

C. What are your fixers?

_____

D. What are your storylines?

_____

E. What other requirements do you have?

_____

F. How do you feel and act in this state?

_____

4. Do the map again, using your bridging awareness practices. Write the same requirement in the oval. Before you continue writing, listen to any background sounds, feel your body's pressure on your seat, sense your feet on the floor, and feel the pen in your hand. Take your time. Once you feel settled, keep feeling the pen in your hand, and start writing. Watch the ink go onto the paper, and listen to any background sounds. For the next few minutes, jot down whatever thoughts pop into your mind.

MOST DIFFICULT TO DEFUSE REQUIREMENT MAP WITH BRIDGING

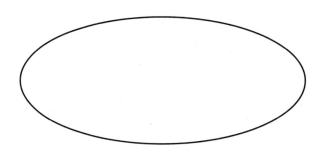

A. How is this map the same as or different from the previous map?

_____

_____

B. How would you feel and act in the same situation with a quiet I-System?

_____

_____

Remember to use your anxiety reduction tools to recognize and defuse your requirements when the situation comes up again.

LET GO OF YOUR REQUIREMENTS

1. Do a What Will Happen If I Let Go of All My Requirements for The World? map. Write your thoughts around the oval for several minutes.

WHAT WILL HAPPEN IF I LET GO OF ALL MY REQUIREMENTS FOR THE WORLD? MAP

WHAT WILL HAPPEN
IF I LET GO OF ALL
MY REQUIREMENTS FOR
THE WORLD?

A. Does the commotion of your I-System leave you feeling weak and anxious, and believing that you will lose control of your life?   Yes _____   No _____

B. Write your level of body tension by each item on the map, using Ø for none, + for minimal, ++ for moderate, or +++ for severe. See the sample map that follows. Next, below, list those items that come with body tension, and identify their underlying requirements:

Item with Body Tension	Requirement

> ### SAMPLE MAP: WHAT WILL HAPPEN IF I LET GO OF ALL MY REQUIREMENTS FOR THE WORLD?

I'll be homebound. +++

The world will be a dangerous place. +++

I'll never be able to do anything. +++

WHAT WILL HAPPEN IF I LET GO OF ALL MY REQUIREMENTS FOR THE WORLD?

Things will go more smoothly. Ø

People will take advantage of me. +++

I'll be anxious all the time. ++

Item with Body Tension	Requirement
The world would be a dangerous place.	*The world should be a safe place.*
I'll be anxious all the time.	*I shouldn't be anxious all the time.*
People will take advantage of me.	*People shouldn't take advantage of me.*

2. Do the map again, this time using your bridging awareness practices. Before you start writing, listen to background sounds, feel your body's pressure on your seat, sense your feet on the floor, and feel the pen in your hand. Take your time. Once you're settled, keep feeling the pen in your hand, and start writing your thoughts. Watch the ink go onto the paper, and listen to background sounds. Write for a couple of minutes.

WHAT WILL HAPPEN IF I LET GO OF ALL MY REQUIREMENTS FOR THE WORLD? MAP WITH BRIDGING

WHAT WILL HAPPEN
IF I LET GO OF ALL MY
REQUIREMENTS FOR
THE WORLD?

What are the differences between the two maps?

_____

_____

_____

_____

Is it getting clearer that having I-System requirements is harmful to you and your world? Requirements limit your ability to deal with other people and situations. When you quiet your I-System, your natural powerful self can respond in an active, attentive, and healthy way in your relationships and situations. You'll be able to face each moment with full access to your inner wellspring of healing, goodness, and wisdom. Your powerful self will be in charge.

APPLY YOUR ANXIETY REDUCTION TOOLS IN YOUR DAILY LIFE

Amy, a twenty-five-year-old office worker in a large company, gradually became unable to function at work because of anxiety. Her frequent trips to the bathroom because of diarrhea, her being easily startled, and her racing anxious thoughts made work a hell for her. After using up most of her sick leave, she took the advice of her primary care physician and sought help. She started mind-body bridging. Her bridging awareness practices relieved her anxiety enough so she could resume working. By mapping her distressing experiences and using other follow-up maps, she saw requirements, such as *No one should slam the door* and *No one should shout.* When these situations would happen, her storylines—*They are angry with me, I could get fired, I can't stand it*—fueled her I-System and led to her symptoms. Using her anxiety reduction tools to defuse her requirements, Amy became able to calm her I-System and do her work. Now a sudden noise may startle her a little bit, but doesn't create anxiety.

Defusing requirements is a key anxiety reduction tool. Remember, using all of your anxiety reduction tools allows you to become good at switching off your I-System. Turning off your anxiety switch gives you access to your powerful self, which functions in the executive mode without anxiety.

Anxiety Reduction Tool

➢ Defuse your requirements for others and for situations.

MBB RATING SCALE: DEFUSE YOUR REQUIREMENTS TO PREVENT ANXIETY

Date: _____

After using the tool in this chapter for several days, check the description that most closely reflects your practice: hardly ever, sometimes, usually, or almost always.

How often do you...	Hardly Ever	Sometimes	Usually	Almost Always
Recognize that requirements always trigger your I-System and limit your powerful self?				
Recognize the requirements that are responsible for your anxiety?				
Prevent anxiety by defusing a requirement?				
See that requirements you have for others or situations trap you, keeping you from being your true self?				
Cut off storylines by using thought labeling and bridging awareness practices?				
Notice the powerless self when it's in charge?				
Experience the powerless self as a myth of the I-System?				
Experience your powerful self functioning in the executive mode, when your I-System is switched off?				
Know it's your natural true self when you are naturally functioning moment by moment (executive-functioning loop)?				
Come to appreciate aspects of your everyday life?				
Experience that you are connected to a wellspring of healing, goodness, and wisdom?				
Find that your relationships have improved?				
Function better at home and at work?				

List three requirements you defused that previously caused a meltdown. How did you deal with the situation(s) in the executive-functioning loop?

_____

_____

_____

CHAPTER 6

BUILD ANXIETY-FREE
RELATIONSHIPS

Discover, Experience, and Apply

Discover how the I-System prevents you from having anxiety-free relationships.

Experience how defusing your requirements for yourself improves your relationships.

Apply your anxiety reduction tools in your daily life.

RELATIONSHIPS, ANXIETY, AND YOUR I-SYSTEM

The requirements of your I-System get you into relationships you shouldn't be in, keep you out of those that are good for you, and, most importantly, create anxiety in your present relationships.

Sharri was anxious about coming home because she dreaded having yet another spat with her husband. When her husband got home first, she would avoid coming into the house and would sit in the driveway for hours. When Sharri finally went into her house, she would quickly walk to the bedroom and isolate herself to avoid any conflict.

Sharri responded rapidly to mind-body bridging as she recognized that her I-System was responsible for her anxiety symptoms. When she quieted her I-System, her mind and body began to settle down. Her How My World Would Look If My Requirements for Others Were Met map helped her to recognize her requirements, *Sam should always be happy to see me, Sam should give me time to unwind when I get home, Sam should not raise his voice,* and *Sam should always support me no matter what.* After completing the map, Sharri had an "aha" moment. She realized it wasn't Sam's behavior that was creating her anxiety; it was her I-System's requirement about how Sam should be. Sharri saw that her anxious thoughts and her avoidance of Sam were due to her anticipating how she would feel when Sam failed to meet her I-System's ideal picture. Her I-System had her convinced she was so powerless that she could only be anxiety-free when Sam was perfect. Now when Sam doesn't smile and greet her, she is disappointed but not devastated. Needless to say, Sharri and Sam are pleased with their improved relationship.

The requirements you have for yourself constantly create inner distress, impair your self-esteem, and interfere with your relationships. You know how painful it is when others don't accept who you are. But what about the pain you put yourself through when you don't accept yourself? Can you imagine the relief you feel when your inner critic is quiet, letting your powerful self be in the driver's seat? When you defuse your persistent self-demands (requirements for yourself), you reduce your anxiety and strengthen the foundations of your relationships. The real stressor creating the anxiety in your relationships is neither you nor the other person, but your active I-System. Once it has been made active by a requirement (*I should be…*), your depressor pulls the rug out from under your self-esteem, making you feel small, weak, vulnerable, and inadequate. Your fixer responds by driving your anxiety-filled behaviors with overactive, never-ending worry and thoughts of how to fix yourself and the world. Your body is full of tension and your thoughts are anxiety-filled. This interferes with your self-esteem, and keeps you from developing healthy relationships. When your I-System is quiet, you clearly see that your troubling thoughts are just thoughts, your body is calm, and you know the truth—you are whole and complete. This is the anxiety-free base for your relationships.

It's vital to remember that defusing requirements like *He shouldn't be so demanding, My wife shouldn't speak to other men,* and *No one should show interest in my partner* doesn't mean you give up your natural expectation that you and your partner behave in an acceptable way. What it does mean is that when your partner acts in a way that used to create your anxiety (because of your requirement), your natural powerful self will now respond to the situation in an appropriate way. If that requirement is not defused, your ability to respond remains controlled by your active I-System.

KEEP THE PAST IN THE PAST

Anxiety has roots in the past. Mind-body bridging does not try to uncover or understand the past; it gives you the tools to heal your anxiety by keeping the past in the past.

1. Do a How I Got to Be the Way I Am map. Around the oval, write how you got to be the way you are. Write for a couple of minutes. A sample map follows.

HOW I GOT TO BE THE WAY I AM MAP

(HOW I GOT TO BE THE
WAY I AM)

A. What is your body tension?

_____

B. What storyline themes run through your map?

_____

_____

C. Describe when and how often you use these storylines—for example, when you feel anxious or calm, when you're sad or happy, or when you're bored or busy:

_____

D. How do you feel and act when the above storylines are active?

_____

The I-System uses stories—positive and negative, about the past and future—to keep you from living in the present. No matter what they are about, storylines tense your body, limit your awareness, and pull you away from being able to take care of yourself and your responsibilities. Storylines stop your mind-body from experiencing the present moment and prevent you from healing your anxiety. Being aware of your storylines quiets your I-System and puts you in the executive-functioning loop, where thoughts of the past are simply thoughts, without the heat and spin of the I-System.

SAMPLE MAP: HOW I GOT TO BE THE WAY I AM

I grew up in foster care.

A lot of pain

Poor school district.

Mom was depressed.

Dad wasn't around much.

It's too difficult to think about.

HOW I GOT TO BE THE WAY I AM

I was fine before my parents divorced.

I always knew Mom loved me, but she didn't show it.

I was physically abused.

I never gave up.

My friends always had my back.

A. What is your body tension? *As I mull over my painful past, my heart starts to beat fast, and I become anxious.*

B. What storyline themes run through your map? *I was a victim.*

C. Describe when and how often you use these storylines: *Whenever things don't go right.*

D. How do you feel and act when the above storylines are active? *I feel irritated and angry and lash out at people.*

2. Do another How I Got to Be the Way I Am map, this time using your bridging awareness practices. Before writing, listen to any background sounds, feel your body's pressure on your seat, sense your feet on the floor, and feel the pen in your hand. After you feel settled, jot around the oval whatever thoughts pop into your mind. Keep listening to background sounds and feeling the pen in your hand. Watch the ink go onto the paper. Write for a couple of minutes.

HOW I GOT TO BE THE WAY I AM MAP WITH BRIDGING

(HOW I GOT TO BE THE WAY I AM)

A. How is this map different from your first How I Got to Be the Way I Am map?

_____

_____

_____

B. What insights have you gained from doing this bridging map?

_____

_____

_____

_____

When you continue to do maps like the one above, your past remains the past.

WHAT STOPS YOU FROM HEALING YOUR ANXIETY

"Being in the moment" has become a popular theme for improving yourself and your relationships. But the problem is not being in the moment, because there has never been a human being who wasn't in the moment. You can only breathe now; you can only act now. Your heart can't pump yesterday's blood or tomorrow's blood; it can only beat right here, right now. It's impossible not to live in the present moment. The problem is that the I-System, when activated by requirements, keeps you in a state of anxiety and pulls you away from experiencing the healing power of your natural self, right here, right now. Let's see how it works.

Do a How I Want to Be Right Here, Right Now map. *Inside* the circle, write how you would like to be right here, right now (for example, *organized, strong, calm, confident, attractive*). Be specific! After you have listed at least six qualities, write the opposite of each quality *outside* the circle. Connect the quality inside the circle with a line to its opposite, outside the circle. If needed, see the sample map that follows.

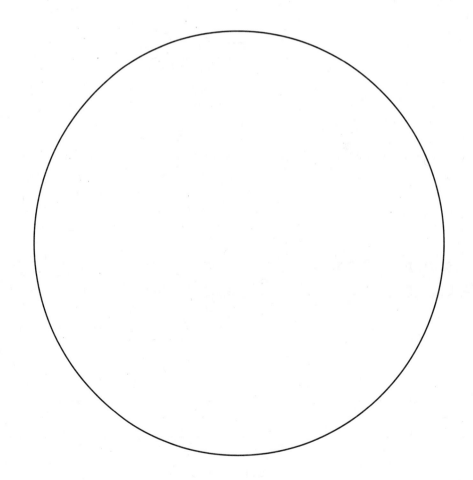

HOW I WANT TO BE RIGHT HERE, RIGHT NOW MAP

SAMPLE MAP: HOW I WANT TO BE RIGHT HERE, RIGHT NOW

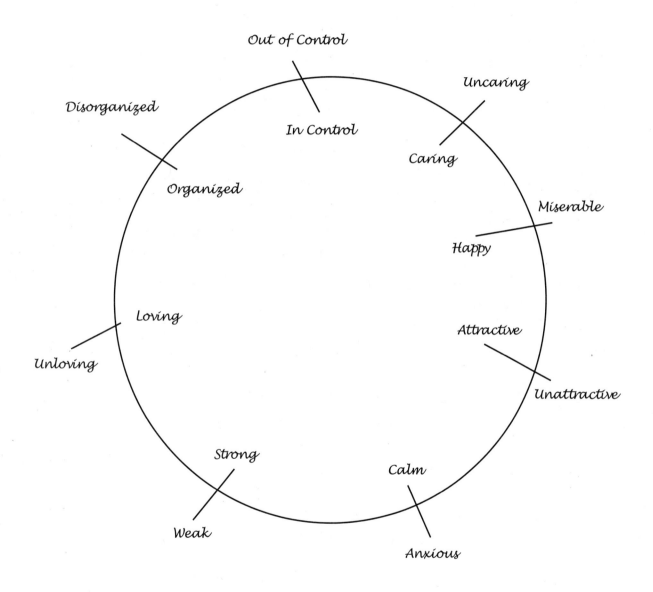

1. How do the qualities *inside* the circle make you feel?

    _____

    _____

    _____

2. How do the qualities *outside* the circle make you feel?

    _____

    _____

    _____

If the qualities *outside* the circle create body tension and negative emotions, they are triggers. Remember, a trigger (an event or thought) is a sign that a requirement has made your I-System active. This means that those opposite qualities (about how you want to be) *inside* the circle are requirements the I-System has created for you. Once your requirement for yourself is defused, the trigger no longer turns on your I-System.

3. From your map, list your triggers and requirements about how you "should" be:

Trigger	Requirement
Being disorganized	*I should be organized.*

When your I-System takes hold of your natural expectation, that expectation turns into a requirement (an ideal picture of who you should be). This creates mind clutter and body tension, and keeps your anxiety going. Your self-esteem suffers, and your relationships are filled with anxiety. Recognizing and defusing the requirements you have for yourself and about how you interact with others is the key to healing your anxiety and improving your relationships.

MIRROR, MIRROR ON THE WALL

Did you know that poor self-image keeps your anxiety going and affects your relationships?

1. Let's do a Mirror map. Find a quiet place and look in a mirror. Before you start writing, really look at yourself for a minute or so. Next, write around the oval any thoughts and feelings that come to mind about what you see. Try not to censor anything. Glance back at the mirror several times and keep writing whatever comes to mind. Describe your body tension at the bottom of the map.

MIRROR MAP

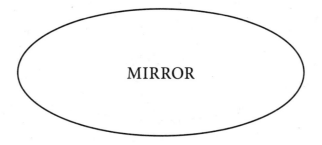

Body Tension: _____

A. Is your I-System active?   Yes _____   No _____

B. What are your storylines?

_____

_____

C. Is your depressor causing you to experience your face as an enemy and making you feel unacceptable?   Yes _____   No _____

D. What are your requirements?

_____

_____

E. How do you feel and act when you don't accept yourself?

_____

2. Do another Mirror map, this time using your bridging awareness practices. Before writing, listen to any background sounds, feel your body's pressure on your seat, sense your feet on the floor, and feel the pen in your hand. Now look in the mirror and keep listening to background sounds. Take your time. After you feel settled, jot around the oval whatever thoughts pop into your mind. Keep listening to background sounds and feeling the pen in your hand. Watch the ink go onto the paper. Write for a couple of minutes.

MIRROR MAP WITH BRIDGING

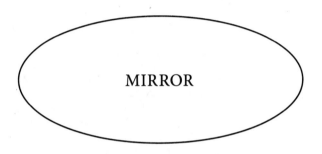

MIRROR

A. How is this map different from your first Mirror map?

_____

_____

B. Did the facial features you see in the mirror change?   Yes _____   No _____

C. Do you now have a new level of self-acceptance?   Yes _____   No _____

D. How do you act when you accept yourself?

_____

Take a good look at your image in the mirror every morning and again at night. Let your thoughts flow freely, and notice your body tension. See the telltale signs of your active I-System. Be aware of your depressor, your fixer, and, most importantly, your requirements for yourself. When you use your bridging awareness practices, the foundation of who you are becomes stable and your emotions balance themselves. Over time observe how your self-image improves without your having to try to fix yourself. This shift in self-acceptance that comes with the continued use of your anxiety reduction tools makes a firm base for anxiety-free relationships.

ANXIETY REDUCTION TOOLS TO IMPROVE YOUR SELF-IMAGE

- *Thought labeling*: When a negative thought pops into your mind, remember, a thought is just a thought. Label your negative thoughts as just thoughts, and return to what you were doing. For example, when *I'll never be good enough* pops into your mind, say to yourself, *I'm having the thought, "I'll never be good enough," and it's just a thought.*

- *Bridging awareness practices*: When you notice negative self-talk and body tension in your life, know that it is a sign that your I-System is switched on, tune in to your senses, and then go back to what you were doing.

- *Storyline awareness*: When you catch yourself going over stories about negative things that have happened to you, notice the repeating themes, recognize them as storylines, and return to the task at hand. Recognize it's the storylines and not your past that are keeping your anxiety going. You are not a victim of your past. Remember, it's not your negative thoughts that get you down or your positive thoughts that pull you up; your storylines (true or false, positive or negative) create mind clutter and fill every cell of your body with tension, keeping the depressor/fixer dance going. When your I-System gets hold of your stories, it takes you away from fully functioning in the present moment, and sets the stage for your anxiety.

- *Mapping*: Use the two-part mind-body maps. The first map helps you find your requirements that reinforce your negative self-beliefs. Noticing your body tension is what helps you find these requirements. Use your bridging awareness practices on the second map to see the truth about negative self-beliefs and return to executive functioning.

- *Mirror mapping*: Doing a daily Mirror map (the last two-part map you just did) builds your self-esteem. After you have noticed a calming of your I-System and an improvement in your self-esteem, do a full-body Mirror map.

- *Defusing requirements*: When you notice body tension and negative self-talk, quiet your I-System, and then find your requirement. For example, if the negative self-talk is *I'm help-less*, the requirement is *I should not be helpless*. When a situation comes up and a thought enters your mind about being helpless and you have signs of body tension, your I-System has been activated by that requirement, impairing your ability to deal with the situation. To defuse the requirement, recognize that your distress is caused by the requirement and not by the situation or your negative thoughts. Once you feel a release of body tension and mind clutter (whether over time or suddenly), you know you have defused your requirement. Your powerful self is back in the driver's seat.

Liz, twenty-one years old, had low self-esteem throughout high school and college. She hated to look in the mirror, and even tried the latest self-esteem improvement method of not looking at herself in a mirror for three months. A girlfriend invited her to a mind-body bridging women's group. After using the introductory anxiety reduction tools, she tried Mirror mapping. After two weeks, she told her group that when she did the second part of the full body map, she was overcome with the experience, "God loves me, I'm acceptable, and I'm lovable."

POWERING YOUR SELF-IMAGE REDUCES ANXIETY AND IMPROVES RELATIONSHIPS

Use your anxiety reduction tools today to keep your negative self-image and self-talk from getting you down, and making you anxious. Then fill out the chart below.

Negative Self-Image	Body Tension	What Anxiety Reduction Tools Did You Use and How	Body Sensations	How Your Behavior Changed after Using Your Tools
I'm not smart enough to get ahead in the world.	Chest tight, shallow breath	Labeled my thoughts. Listened to hum of air conditioner.	Chest and breathing relaxed	Wasn't as depressed. Accomplished a lot on the job today.
I'm unlovable.	Gut cramps	I immediately recognized the thought, "I should be lovable" as a requirement.	Calmer	"Light came on," day went smoothly, and I wasn't defensive or angry.

Your I-System requirements about how you "should be" are getting in the way of your self-image. These requirements keep you from believing and trusting in who you are, right here and now. Recall that you will never be smart enough, attractive enough, or calm enough to satisfy a requirement. When the requirement isn't satisfied, your I-System heats up with negative thoughts and body tensions. This affects not only how you feel about yourself, but also how you act in your relationships. No matter who you are or what you have been through, your mind-body anxiety reduction tools can strengthen your self-image, heal your anxiety, and improve your relationships.

REQUIREMENTS FOR YOURSELF KEEP YOU FROM HEALING ANXIETY

1. List three situations from the last several days where your requirements for yourself—for example, *I should know the answer when my boss asks me a question, I should be home on time, I shouldn't be alone, I shouldn't make a mistake*—activated your I-System.

Situation	Requirement for Yourself
At our morning meeting, my boss asked me a question.	I should know the answer when my boss asks me a question.

2. Fill out this chart based on what you listed in the chart above:

Body Tension and Its Progression When Your Requirement Is Met	Body Tension and Its Progression When Your Requirement Is *Not* Met
Stomach tight, foot jiggles, hands grip chair arms tightly	Face hot, dry mouth, pressure builds in chest

3. Fill out the next chart for each requirement from the previous one:

Storylines When Meeting Requirement	Storylines When Not Meeting Requirement
It's a relief, It's over, What will happen next time, It's always the same.	*I'll never have all the answers, I'm stupid, I may lose my job.*

4. Fill out the next chart using the same requirements:

Your Behavior When Meeting Requirement	Your Behavior When Not Meeting Requirement
Felt relieved, but worried about next time.	*Anxious and depressed all day. Made mistakes.*

The I-System has you between a rock and a hard place. When your requirements for yourself aren't met, your depressor moves into the driver's seat, leaving you powerless and anxious. Even when you are able to meet your requirements, the fixer moves into the driver's seat, and enough is never enough. Your anxiety still isn't settled. It's not a matter of meeting or not meeting your requirements, but one of defusing them. When your requirements are defused, your powerful self is in the driver's seat, and you naturally take the right action moment by moment.

5. Using your bridging awareness practices, listen to background sounds, feel your body's pressure on your seat, sense your feet on the floor, and feel the pen in your hand. When you're settled, label your thoughts and go over each requirement you listed in the first chart in this exercise. What has happened to each of the requirements after mind-body bridging?

Requirement One:

_____

_____

_____

Requirement Two:

_____

_____

_____

Requirement Three:

_____

_____

_____

YOUR EVERYDAY RELATIONSHIPS

Now that you know how critical it is for your self-esteem and well-being that you have a quiet I-System, it's time to tackle your relationships. We all have natural hopes and desires for ourselves and others (to be respectful, dependable, supportive, honest, helpful, and so forth). Each of us uses these natural expectations to guide us as we interact with others. When the I-System takes hold of these expectations and makes them requirements, they harm our relationships, close off our natural executive functioning, and limit our ability to relate to others.

Let's look at what happens when your natural expectations for yourself are turned into requirements, and examine how they harm your relationships and lower your self-esteem. This exercise is about the requirements you have for yourself in your relationships with coworkers, in-laws, neighbors, grocery clerks, and so on (for example, *I shouldn't be anxious when I host the neighborhood potluck, I should get along with all of my coworkers, I should like my mother-in-law*).

Answer the following questions:

1. My relationship with _____

A. What natural expectations do you have for yourself in this relationship? Example: *I should set better boundaries with my friend.*

B. How do you feel and act, and what is your body tension when you don't follow through? Example: *I get anxious and worry about the relationship.*

C. What are your requirements about this relationship?

D. Describe how your anxiety reduction tools to defuse your requirements and change this relationship.

2. List your natural expectations for yourself in other everyday relationships; be as specific as possible. Note if they have been made into requirements.

Natural Expectation	Body Tension If Expectation Is Not Met	Is It Now A Requirement?
I want to be a good friend.	*Knot in stomach, shoulders tight*	*Yes*
Be polite to the grocery clerk.	*None*	*No*

When your requirement isn't met, you are in distress, with your I-System creating mind clutter and body tension. Recognize your requirements and use your anxiety reduction tools to defuse them. When your natural expectation isn't met, you feel let down, but you are able to handle the situation without undue worry or anxiety.

YOUR MOST IMPORTANT RELATIONSHIP

1. Map your expectations for yourself in your most important relationship. Write the person's name in the oval. Around the oval, write your thoughts about how you should be in that relationship (for example, *I should be attractive, I shouldn't upset him when he's tired, I should make him happy*). There's no right or wrong. Be specific and work quickly for the next few minutes.

HOW I SHOULD BE IN MY MOST IMPORTANT RELATIONSHIP MAP

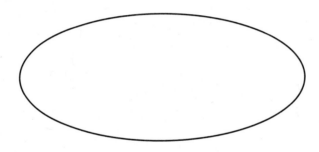

Look at each item and notice any body tension you have when you think about meeting that expectation for how you should be in that relationship. Look again at each item and notice your body tension when you think about *not* meeting that expectation. Thoughts that come with body tension are your requirements.

For each item with body tension, describe how you act when you don't meet that requirement:

_____

_____

_____

_____

2. Do the map again, writing the person's name in the oval. Before you continue writing, listen to background sounds, feel your body's pressure on your seat, sense your feet on the floor, and feel the pen in your hand. Take your time. Once you're settled, keep feeling the pen in your hand, and start writing any thoughts that come to mind about that relationship. As you write, keep paying attention to background sounds, feeling the pen in your hand, and watching the ink go onto the paper. Write for a couple of minutes.

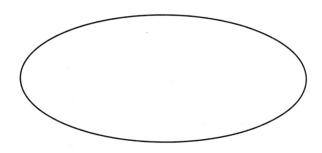

HOW I SHOULD BE IN MY MOST IMPORTANT RELATIONSHIP MAP WITH BRIDGING

A. In this mind-body state, how do you act?

_____

_____

B. How can this map help you in your relationship?

_____

_____

The release of body tension means you have moved from the I-System loop into the executive-functioning loop (see figure 5.1), where your powerful self acts in a natural way. You still have thoughts or natural expectations about how you should be in your relationship, but this release of body tension frees you to act in a different way.

When you let go of your requirements, your active I-System is switched off and your ability to relate to others is changed forever.

TRANSFORM YOUR MOST IMPORTANT RELATIONSHIP

You have been building a foundation for your relationship by defusing your requirements for yourself. Now it's time to focus on the requirements you have for the person who is most important to you.

1. Do a map of how you think the person most important to you should act. Write that person's name in the oval. Around the oval, write your thoughts for how you want that person to act. Write for a couple of minutes.

HOW THE PERSON MOST IMPORTANT TO ME SHOULD ACT MAP

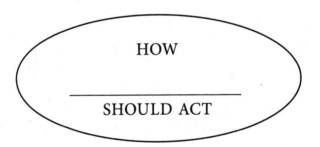

Look back over the items on the map and label your requirements with an "R." Next, under each requirement, write what storylines ("SL") you have when the other person does not meet that requirement. Below each thought, note whatever body tension ("BT") you have when the other person doesn't meet your requirement. Take your time doing this map. See the sample map that follows.

SAMPLE MAP: HOW THE PERSON MOST IMPORTANT TO ME SHOULD ACT

(R) *He needs to do more around the house.*

(SL) *I do all the work, and it takes a lot to make the house perfect, and he knows how much I need to have a clean house.*

(BT) *Tight chest*

(R) *He should take me out to eat more often.*

(SL) *He's ashamed of me.*

(BT) *Chest hurts*

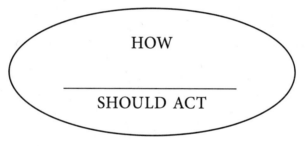

(R) *She should respect how hard I work.*

(SL) *I don't get any slack; I hate conflict and always lose.*

(BT) *Shoulders tight*

(R) *He should show me how attractive I am.*

(SL) *I saw him looking at that woman at the bar.*

(BT) *Stomachache*

R = Requirement

SL = Storyline when requirement is unfulfilled

BT = Body tension when requirement is unfulfilled

A. For each item on your map, fill out the following chart:

Requirement	How Do You Feel and Act When Your Important Other Doesn't Meet Your Requirement?	How Does It Affect Your Relationship?
He should respect how hard I work.	*Withdraw, I worry that I am not good enough for him, I go to the bar with a friend.*	*Creates distance and guilty feelings.*

B. Now, using your bridging awareness practices and thought labeling, when you feel settled, go back over your relationship requirements from the chart above and fill out the chart below.

Requirement	How Do You Act When Your Important Other Doesn't Meet Your Requirement?	How Does It Affect Your Relationship?
He should respect how hard I work.	*Disappointed, but can talk to him.*	*Makes us closer.*

When there is a release of body tension, it shows that you are ready to defuse your requirement when the situation comes up again.

2. Write the name of the person from the previous map in the oval below. Next, choose the requirement that still causes you the most distress when it's not met (for example, *He should respect how hard I work*) and write that on the line below. Now write your thoughts around the oval for a couple of minutes, describing how things would look if that person did meet that requirement. Use as much detail as possible. For example, if the requirement is *He should respect how hard I work*, you might write, *He would not be critical*, *He would not raise his voice*, or *He would tell me how much he loves me*.

> ## HOW THINGS WOULD LOOK IF MY REQUIREMENT WERE MET MAP

Requirement that causes me the most distress: _____

HOW THINGS WOULD
LOOK IF
_____
MET MY REQUIREMENT

A. Do you really think this will happen?   Yes _____   No _____

B. Do you recognize that an active I-System will keep creating requirements for you and your relationship?   Yes _____   No _____

Many people smile when doing this map, because they see clearly how the I-System works. They see that when they defuse their requirements, they can handle personal boundaries and basic rights from a position of strength and without anxiety.

WHO IS STILL CREATING ANXIETY FOR YOU?

Mind-body bridging is not about finding out how you should relate to others; it *is* about finding out how the I-System restricts you and your relationships.

1. Do a requirement map for someone who is still creating anxiety for you. In the oval, write the name of the person who continues to trouble you the most. Around the oval, write your expectations for how that person should act. Write for a couple of minutes.

PERSON CREATING ANXIETY MAP

A. Next, under each item on the map, list any body tension you have when the other person does *not* meet that expectation. Those items are requirements.

B. Describe how the fixer and depressor are dancing in this relationship.

_____

_____

C. What are your storylines?

_____

_____

D. In this mind-body state, how do you feel and act?

_____

2. Do the map again, this time using your bridging awareness practices. Write the same person's name in the oval. Before you continue writing, listen to background sounds, feel your body's pressure on your seat, sense your feet on the floor, and feel the pen in your hand. Take your time. Once you're settled, keep feeling the pen in your hand and start writing any thoughts that come to mind about how that person should act. Watch the ink go onto the paper and keep listening to background sounds. Write for a couple of minutes.

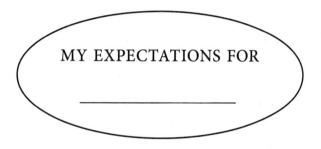

PERSON CREATING ANXIETY MAP WITH BRIDGING

MY EXPECTATIONS FOR

_____

A. How is this map different from the previous map?

_____

B. What body sensations do you have when you imagine that person not doing what you wrote down on this map? The absence of body tension means that the item is not a requirement and that it is a natural expectation.

_____

C. In this mind-body state, how do you feel and act?

_____

D. When your I-System is switched off, your natural goals and expectations do not become pressure-driven requirements. Go back to the previous map and use your anxiety reduction tools on any remaining requirements you had for that person. Do this map as often as needed.

When you recognize and defuse requirements you have for both yourself and others, your powerful self, with its whole range of experiences, emotions, and gifts, enters into each and every relationship. There is no instruction manual for keeping relationships free of anxiety, only the golden key: an I-System at rest.

APPLY THE TOOLS IN YOUR DAILY LIFE

When you defuse requirements for yourself, you are released from the grip of an active I-System, and you have the power to build an anxiety-free foundation for your relationships. You now have access to your powerful self in the executive mode, which acts in a healthy and appropriate way.

Tools to Defuse Requirements for Yourself

1. Be aware of the first signs that your I-System has been switched on (body tension, self-critical or anxious thoughts, or storylines). This will prompt you to look for the hidden requirement.

2. Use your thought labeling and bridging awareness practice tools to stop the uproar of the I-System.

3. Recognize that it's your requirement for yourself, not the other person or the situation, that's causing your distress and anxiety.

4. Use your anxiety reduction tools to find and defuse your requirement.

5. You'll know you have defused the requirement when you feel a release of body tension and self-critical mind clutter. When the situation comes up again, your powerful self will be in the driver's seat, and you'll be able to deal with it in a calm and appropriate way.

As you defuse your requirements for yourself, you create the power to improve your relationships and heal your anxiety. When you defuse both sets of your requirements (for how you and the other person should be), your powerful self, in the executive mode, will naturally build relationships that are healthy and free of anxiety.

Anxiety Reduction Tools

➢ Defuse your requirements for yourself.

➢ Defuse your requirements for your relationships.

➢ Mirror mapping

MBB RATING SCALE: BUILD ANXIETY-FREE RELATIONSHIPS

Date: _____

After using the tools in this chapter for several days, check the description that most closely reflects your practice: hardly ever, sometimes, usually, or almost always.

How often do you...	Hardly Ever	Sometimes	Usually	Almost Always
Notice that requirements always switch on your I-System, causing stress in your relationships?				
Notice that requirements keep your negative self-image going?				
Improve relationships by defusing requirements?				
See that your requirements for yourself trap you and keep your anxiety going?				
Experience yourself as far more than who you thought you were?				
Notice that all you need to do to act from executive functioning is quiet your I-System?				
Notice when your powerless self is in the driver's seat?				
Experience your powerless self as a myth of the I-System?				
Recognize when you are in executive-functioning mode?				
Appreciate your powerful self (who you are when you function naturally moment by moment)?				
See everyday life in a new light by having a quiet I-System?				
Notice yourself connected to your wellspring of healing, goodness, and wisdom?				
Notice that your relationships have improved?				
Function better at home and at work?				
Notice your self-esteem increasing?				

List three requirements for yourself in your relationship that used to make you anxious and that you now deal with by releasing the I-System's tension and letting yourself function in the executive mode:

_____

_____

_____

CHAPTER 7

MASTER YOUR EMOTIONS

Discover, Experience, and Apply

Discover how your I-System causes your emotions to get out of control.

Experience how calming the I-System allows you to be in charge of your emotions.

Apply your anxiety reduction tools in your daily life.

EMOTIONS AND THE I-SYSTEM

Emotions are your personal experience of various special and unique mind-body states. All your emotions, including fear and anxiety, are originally from executive functioning. When the I-System is at rest, your emotions are mind-body facts that naturally allow you to live your best life. Your natural emotions along with your actions express your powerful self.

When your I-System is active, the depressor and fixer corrupt each natural emotion. These altered emotions create suffering, misery, and distress. The depressor takes natural emotions like sadness, disappointment, guilt, and remorse, and creates a heavy, painful, slowed down body with negative storylines. These altered emotions are no longer helpful; they become a burden weighing down and restricting your life. On the other hand, the fixer takes natural emotions like fear, anxiety, and anger, and stirs up your body and mind. These altered emotions captured by the I-System cause you to become overly fearful, anxious, or angry, and create a state where you are bound to overreact. The bottom line is that the I-System causes these altered emotions to rule you. Your natural emotions, which are there to add color and vitality to your life, are corrupted by the I-System and become the boss of your daily life. By using your anxiety reduction tools to quiet your I-System, your emotions automatically revert back to their natural, healthy state.

In mind-body bridging the crucial factor in healing your anxiety is not recognizing the difference between worry, fear, and anxiety, but recognizing whether or not your I-System is switched on or off. When your I-System is switched off, your naturally expanded awareness and wisdom will guide your behavior in all your activities of daily living. The expert in your life is sitting in your chair right here, right now.

A health care professional with an anxiety disorder failed her licensing exam. She suffered from stomachaches, jitters, and fears of failing whenever she thought about the exam and decided she would never take the exam again. Three years later she was assigned a new supervisor, who was certified in mind-body bridging and began working with her. She discovered that it was not her physical or emotional problems that were holding her back; it was her depressor/fixer cycle keeping her I-System in control of her emotions. A series of mind-body maps led her to uncover one requirement after another. Soon she had a plan, and three months after incorporating mind-body bridging into her life, she retook and passed the exam.

In this chapter you will see how your natural emotions get captured by the I-System, and how you can take charge of your emotional life again with your powerful self in the driver's seat. You will also learn an advanced mapping practice called *bubble mapping*. This simple and effective tool gives you the ability to discover additional requirements that are activating your I-System while mapping. When your I-System is at rest, your emotions naturally regulate and your anxiety automatically subsides.

EMOTIONS: ASSETS OR LIABILITIES

1. Do an Emotion map. In the oval, write the emotion that's causing you the most difficulties in your life (for example, *worry, sadness, guilt, jealousy, love, joy,* or *happiness*). Around the oval, write your thoughts for a couple of minutes, without editing them.

EMOTION MAP

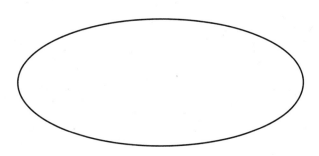

A. Mull over each item. Under each one, write your associated body tension and storylines.

B. Place a "D" next to each item that has depressor activity, and an "F" next to each item that has fixer activity. For example, if the item *I'll never be okay* has a lot of negative storylines and your body feels weighed down, it has depressor activity. If the item *The way he looks at other women* has a lot of pressure-driven storylines like *What is he thinking? What is he doing?* and your body feels anxious and tense, the item has fixer activity.

C. How do you feel and act in this state?

Whenever an emotion is associated with pressure-driven storylines and an overly worked-up or sloweddown body, that emotion has been captured by the I-System.

2. Do the map again, writing the same emotion in the oval. Before you start writing, listen to background sounds and feel your body's pressure on your seat, your feet on the floor, and the pen in your hand. Take your time. Once you are settled, keep feeling the pen in your hand as you start writing. Watch the ink go onto the paper and listen to background sounds. For the next few minutes, jot down any thoughts that come to mind.

EMOTION MAP WITH BRIDGING

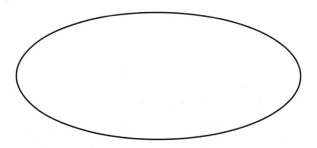

How does your body feel, and how do you act in this state?

_____

_____

The emotions on this map, which are not associated with body tension, come from your powerful self.

Every single emotion you will ever experience arises from your reservoir of natural functioning. When the I-System captures that emotion, it either adds on to it (*so anxious that you can't sleep or take care of your responsibilities*) or takes away from it (*so numb that you are unable to take care of yourself or others*).

During the day, whenever your emotions seem to be getting the best of you, use your bridging awareness practices and thought labeling to recognize the two parts of emotions: *thoughts* and *body sensations*. As you have learned from your bridging map, a calmer mind and body allow you to experience your emotions without your I-System creating anxiety. This puts your natural powerful self in the driver's seat. Try it right now. Recall an emotion-filled situation, listen to background sounds, and notice what happens to your body. As your body settles, your emotions become natural functioning, and your anxiety calms down naturally.

WHO RUNS YOUR LIFE: YOU OR YOUR EMOTIONS?

When you are in charge of your emotions, you bring harmony and balance to your daily life. As long as your I-System is quiet, your powerful self is able to deal with the strongest emotions, such as anxiety, hate, greed, jealousy, shame, guilt, love, happiness, and joy. It's not about the quality or quantity of the emotion; it's simply about who's in charge: your limited, powerless self or your expansive, powerful self. No matter how deep your love is or how strong your other emotions are, if your I-System is in charge, it will taint how you express and experience your emotions.

1. Go back over your past. List three experiences where positive emotions caused you to make poor decisions, not take good care of yourself, or become full of anxiety.

Experience	Positive Emotion
Fell in love, I would text him day and night, and I felt anxious if he didn't text me right back.	*Love*

2. List three experiences you had where negative emotions caused you to make poor decisions and not take good care of yourself.

Experience	Negative Emotion
My in-laws were coming for a visit.	*Anxiety*

POSITIVE EMOTIONAL EXPERIENCE

1. From your prior list, select the positive emotion that resulted in the most anxiety and write it in the oval. Take a couple of minutes to write your thoughts around the oval. Work quickly without editing your thoughts.

STRONGEST POSITIVE EMOTION MAP

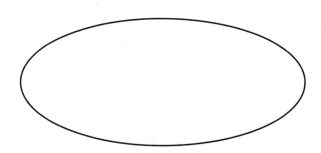

A. Mull over each item. Under each one, write your associated body tension and storylines.

B. Place a "D" next to each item that has depressor activity, and an "F" next to each item that has fixer activity.

C. What are your requirements?

_____

_____

_____

2. Do this map again. Write the same positive emotion in the oval. Before you continue writing, listen to any background sounds, feel your body's pressure on your seat, sense your feet on the floor, and feel the pen in your hand. Take your time. Once you feel settled, keep feeling the pen in your hand and start writing. Watch the ink go onto the paper, and listen to any background sounds. For the next few minutes, jot down whatever thoughts pop into your mind.

STRONGEST POSITIVE EMOTION MAP WITH BRIDGING

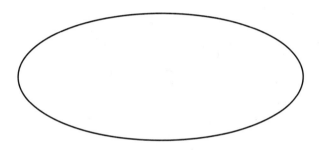

A. What are the differences between the two maps?

_____

_____

B. What anxiety reduction tools will you use to defuse the rest of your requirements on the first map in the exercise?

_____

C. Do you see how your I-System causes anxiety, not your emotions?   Yes _____   No _____

When an intense emotion arises it is important to recognize if your powerful self is experiencing it, or if the I-System's fixer or depressor are involved. If the emotion has been grabbed by the I-System, listen to the background sounds, label your thoughts, and recognize your storylines. It's also helpful to map out your requirements connected to this captured emotion. Switching off the I-System lets each emotion return to natural functioning and automatically reduces anxiety.

NEGATIVE EMOTIONAL EXPERIENCE

1. From the earlier list, select the negative emotion that caused you the most anxiety and write it in the oval. Write your thoughts around the oval for a couple of minutes.

STRONGEST NEGATIVE EMOTION MAP

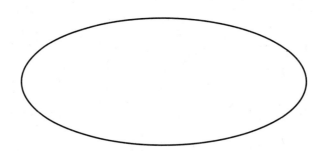

A. Mull over each item. Under each one, write your associated body tension and storylines.

B. Place a "D" next to each item that has depressor activity, and an "F" next to each item that has fixer activity.

C. What are your requirements?

_____

_____

_____

2. Do this map again. Write the same negative emotion in the oval. Before you continue writing, use your bridging awareness practices. Listen to background sounds and feel your body's pressure on your seat, your feet on the floor, and the pen in your hand. Take your time. Once you are settled, keep feeling the pen in your hand as you start writing. Watch the ink go onto the paper, and listen to background sounds. For the next few minutes, jot down any thoughts that come to mind.

STRONGEST NEGATIVE EMOTION MAP WITH BRIDGING

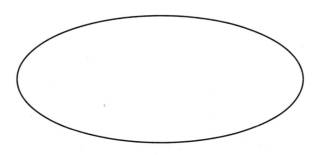

A. What are the differences between the two maps?

_____

_____

B. Is your I-System or your powerful self in charge?

_____

C. What anxiety reduction tools will you use to defuse the remaining requirements on the first map in the exercise?

_____

_____

D. Do you see how your I-System causes anxiety, not your emotions?   Yes _____   No _____

    As this map shows, your negative emotions are not your enemy. When you are in the executive mode, you experience your emotions without feeling anxious. Your powerful self automatically results in mind-body well-being.

STAY CALM WHEN THE BOTTOM FALLS OUT

1. We have all had situations where we felt comfortable that everything was under control and then something suddenly happened that caused the bottom to fall out. Fill out the chart below, and list some of those situations.

Troubling Situation	Your Reaction	Requirement
My partner told me I'm fat.	Could not think straight. Felt like I was unattractive and not good enough. Stayed away from him.	He shouldn't tell me I'm fat.
Invitation to a high school reunion.	Became worried about what my classmates would think of me, so I couldn't sleep. Only felt better when I decided not to go.	My classmates should think I have it all together. I shouldn't have to go to the high school reunion.
Meeting with big boss who is visiting our facility.	My heart started pounding, my hands shaking. When I thought about work I couldn't think straight. Worried he would see how insecure I am. Was tempted to call in sick.	I shouldn't have to meet him. I shouldn't be a nervous wreck.

It's crucial to be aware of when you first begin to feel anxious, or see the first signs of an active I-System. When you use your anxiety reduction tools right away, you stop your I-System from taking control and prevent your emotions from being ruled by it.

2. From the prior chart, choose the most troubling situation that created the most anxiety. Write that situation in the oval. Around the oval, write your thoughts for a couple of minutes without editing them.

BOTTOM FALLS OUT MAP

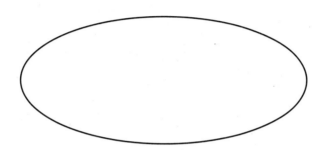

A. What is your body tension and how does it progress?

_____

B. List your depressor/fixer storylines:

_____

_____

_____

C. Look at your map again. Draw a circle (bubble) around the thought that has the *most* body tension. Take a few minutes to write your thoughts around that bubbled item. "Bubble" mapping helps you uncover more of your requirements. Bubble map other troubling thoughts on this map.

D. Identify and list as many requirements as you can:

_____

_____

_____

3. Do the map again, writing the same troubling situation in the oval. Before you continue writing, listen to background sounds and feel your body's pressure on your seat, your feet on the floor, and the pen in your hand. Take your time. Once you are settled, keep feeling the pen in your hand as you start writing. Watch the ink go onto the paper and listen to background sounds. For the next few minutes, jot down any thoughts that come to mind.

BOTTOM FALLS OUT MAP WITH BRIDGING

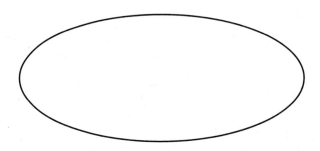

A. What's your mind-body state after bridging, and how do you act in this state?

_____

_____

B. How did your attempt to defuse your remaining requirements go?

_____

_____

Remember, for those requirements that are hard to defuse, find and break down the large requirement into smaller ones. For example, take the requirement *He should love me*. You know what your requirement is, but you're having trouble defusing it. So ask yourself, *What does that requirement look like?* For example: *He should smile when he sees me, He shouldn't go out with the boys so often, He shouldn't get angry with me, He shouldn't make that face at me, He should always compliment me, He should hold my hand in public*. These more detailed requirements are easier to work with and defuse. When you defuse them, the requirement that was hard to defuse (*He should love me*) will defuse on its own.

FEAR

1. Throughout the day, notice the events (for example, *My coworker was fired* or *I'm going to propose*) that led you to become fearful. Recognize the underlying requirement (*I shouldn't lose my job*, *She should say yes*).

Event	Fear	Requirement
Coworker was fired.	I could be fired next.	I shouldn't lose my job.
Marriage proposal.	I'll mess it up, She'll say no.	She should say yes.
Bess's party.	I won't fit in, I'll stand out from everyone else.	I should fit in.
I recognized a problem at work and have a solution.	I might look stupid if I don't say it right.	I should be able to present it clearly. They should adopt my solution.

2. Think back over the past month and list the three greatest fears that affected your activities. Find and list the hidden requirements for each:

_____

_____

_____

3. Do a Fear map, writing your greatest fear in the oval. Write your thoughts around the oval for a couple of minutes without editing them.

```
┌─────────────────────────────────────────────────────────────┐
│                         FEAR MAP                             │
└─────────────────────────────────────────────────────────────┘
```

A. Note the body tension associated with each item and draw a bubble around the thought that brings the most body tension. Take a few minutes to scatter more thoughts around the bubbled item. Bubble map any other troubling items.

B. List your depressor/fixer storylines:

_____

_____

C. Identify and list as many requirements as you can:

_____

_____

_____

Fear is a natural emotion from executive functioning that alerts you to possible danger. Remember that fear, like other emotions, has two parts: a thought and a body sensation. When the I-System captures your fear, it convinces you that you can't cope and fills you with paralyzing distress, making you a victim of your fear. Fighting fear never works because your depressor/fixer takes over and creates even more distress and impaired ability to respond to the situation.

4. Do this map again, writing the same fear in the oval. Before you start writing, listen to background sounds and feel your body's pressure on your seat, your feet on the floor, and the pen in your hand. Take your time. Once you are settled, keep feeling the pen in your hand as you start writing. Watch the ink go onto the paper and listen to background sounds. For the next few minutes, jot down any thoughts that come to mind.

FEAR MAP WITH BRIDGING

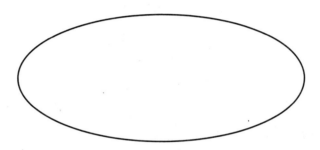

A. What's your mind-body state on this map, compared to the previous one?

_____

_____

B. How would you act differently in this state?

_____

_____

C. Do you think you can defuse your requirements from the previous map the next time the situation comes up?   Yes _____   No _____

In mind-body bridging, being fearless doesn't mean you have no fear. Fear is a natural emotion from executive functioning. Being fearless means that your I-System has not paralyzed your natural ability to deal with the situation that evoked the fear. To control the I-System's influence on your fear, defuse the underlying requirements. When you defuse requirements, rather than reacting to a fearful situation, you deal with the situation with your powerful self in charge.

BEFRIEND ANXIETY

1. Now that you have a solid foundation of mind-body bridging in your daily life, let's befriend your most stubborn anxiety symptom. Before you do this advanced map, be in a quiet place where you can have fifteen minutes of uninterrupted time. Take a few moments to consider your most stubborn anxiety symptom. Write that symptom in the oval. Write your thoughts around the oval. Take your time. Describe your body tension at the bottom of the map.

MY MOST STUBBORN ANXIETY SYMPTOM MAP

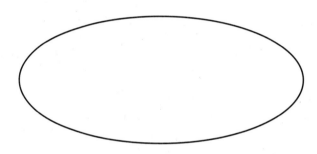

Body Tension: _____

A. Looking at your map, list the signs of your active I-System (requirements, depressor/fixer, storylines):

_____

_____

_____

B. Take the next five to ten minutes to befriend your map. To do that, listen to background sounds and feel your body's pressure on your seat, your feet on the floor, and the pen in your hand. When you become settled, go over each item on your map gently and kindly until your mind and body do not overreact to the item. If an item causes tension, use thought labeling. When you can review your entire map without body tension or anxiety, your map has been befriended.

MASTER YOUR EMOTIONS

2. Do this map again, writing the same thing in the oval. Before you start writing, use your bridging awareness practices. Listen to background sounds and feel your body's pressure on your seat, your feet on the floor, and the pen in your hand. Take your time. Once you are settled, keep feeling the pen in your hand as you start writing. Watch the ink go onto the paper and listen to background sounds. For the next few minutes, jot down any thoughts that come to mind.

MY MOST STUBBORN ANXIETY SYMPTOM MAP WITH BRIDGING

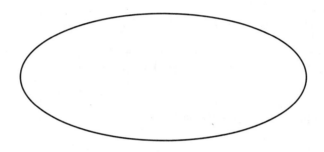

A. What do you notice that's different on this map?

_____

_____

B. When the requirements on your previous map come up again in your life, how are you going to defuse them?

_____

_____

C. Does the symptom in the oval still create anxiety and disconnect you from your powerful self? Yes _____ No _____

D. Is your powerful self always within you, no matter what? Yes _____ No _____

E. For other remaining anxiety symptoms, please repeat this two-part map until you have befriended those anxiety symptoms as well.

AWARENESS TOOLS TO BEFRIEND ANXIETY

Thinking, body sensations, and all emotions (including anxiety) are only problems when your I-System is active and in control. Thinking, body sensations, and anxiety are not your enemies! But when you push them away, deny them, or declare a state of war with them, it only reinforces the I-System's control. The roots of your anxiety become protected and preserved by the I-System, and your body and mind are controlled by your anxiety symptoms. When you befriend painful thoughts, body sensations, emotions, and anxiety symptoms, a natural healing process begins to take place. Here are the powerful awareness tools to befriend anxiety.

1. In any situation, become aware of the early signs of an active I-System—unpleasantly stirred up body sensations, mental urgency, and spinning negative or anxious storylines—and recognize when your depressor/fixer is beginning to take control.

2. Use bridging awareness practices and thought labeling to calm down your I-System.

3. Use your powerful self's awareness to notice any stories that the fixer or depressor may spin. These storylines impair your ability to act, and add even more anxiety.

4. Without judging, gently and patiently uncover the depressor activity that is reinforcing your unpleasant body sensations and negative feelings about yourself.

5. Open your awareness to all of your sights, sounds, and body sensations as well as your anxiety symptom. This awareness interrupts your I-System from taking control.

6. Recognize and defuse the requirements that activated your anxiety symptom. (Mapping helps.)

7. Be aware that it's not the activity you are doing but who's doing it that is important. If it is your I-System's powerless self, your anxiety symptoms will never be resolved. If it's your powerful self, functioning in the executive mode, your anxiety will heal and your activities will be anxiety-free.

Thinking, body sensations, and emotions are a natural part of life. When you become aware that an emotion (like anxiety) has been captured by the I-System, you have a choice to make: use and embrace the emotion as an ally that signals to you that your I-System is switched on, or reject the information and let your I-System be in control. Your powerful self accepts "you" without judging whether you or the emotion are good or bad, friend or foe. This nonjudgmental awareness automatically switches off your I-System and stops the symptom in its tracks. When you befriend anxiety by expanding your awareness, the unsettling symptom loses its power over you. This state of expanded awareness means that your requirements are not active. Your powerful self in the executive mode, with all its healing abilities, creates a balanced mind-body state that allows you to live your best life.

RESTORING NATURAL EMOTIONS

Fran, when in her teens, was responsible for a car accident where her passenger was injured. When her sons no longer needed car seats, she became fearful and excessively worried about them being in the car. When she took them to school, Fran would become so emotionally distraught that she insisted that the boys wear protective helmets whenever they were in a car. She defended her actions as *"It calms me down when I know they are protected. It's just me."*

Soon after starting mind-body bridging, Fran found that using her bridging awareness practices and thought labeling helped her calm her emotions when she drove the car. With this calming emotional space, her overall level of anxiety began to decrease. Next she did a Fearful Situation map about driving in the car. Fran discovered how her storylines about "what if" were responsible for her excessive fears about what might happen to her boys. She recognized that her depressor (feelings of helplessness) was behind the fixer (*I have to protect them any way I can*) and was driving her to insist on the boys wearing helmets. She found her requirements (*I should be in control, I should be a good parent, My children should be safe in a car*) and began to defuse them in real time. As she continued to use her anxiety reduction tools, Fran's excessive worrying and fears subsided, her concerns about safety became appropriate, and with her newfound calm, she became a safer driver. The helmets went back where they belonged, and were used only when riding bikes.

Whenever your emotions make you feel unsettled or overwhelmed, know that it's not "just you." It's your I-System that has taken over your natural emotion and caused your turmoil. It's important to see how the depressor and fixer affect your natural emotions. When the depressor is interfering with your emotion, it is usually easier to recognize because of the negative storylines and the heavy, unpleasant feeling in your body. However, if the fixer is responsible, it is not always as easy to recognize because the fixer tries to mask over the unpleasant thoughts and body sensations. The following are some examples of how the fixer works.

a) It takes your natural emotion of jealousy, which is originally a signal for you to pay attention to your relationship, and converts it to an out-of-control preoccupation. Because the fixer justifies this unhealthy emotion and behavior with storylines, it is more difficult to recognize.

b) The fixer takes your natural emotion of anxiety, which, in its untainted state, signals you to pay attention to something that is going on in your life, and revs it up into a panic attack. Because the fixer has your mind and body so wound up and disturbed, you feel and act as if a panic reaction is your only choice. When the I-System is quiet, the natural anxiety (thoughts and body sensations) enters your expanded awareness. Your powerful self in the executive mode acknowledges the signal and deals appropriately with it.

c) Lastly, when your natural emotion of happiness becomes filled with anxiety and fears of losing that pleasant state, it's the fixer making you believe that happiness should last forever.

Once you become aware of how the depressor and fixer are taking over, know that your emotion has become tied to a requirement. When you realize there is an underlying requirement (*There shouldn't be so many people at the mall, I should be able to talk comfortably in front of a group, I should be perfect*), the power of the I-System is automatically reduced. By recognizing and defusing the requirement (mapping helps), your emotions become more appropriate and your shift into executive functioning prepares you to deal with the situation as it is.

APPLY THE TOOLS IN YOUR DAILY LIFE

You now know that all emotions are natural. Whenever emotions get out of hand, it's always due to a requirement that you are currently unaware of. The depressor and fixer have added on to or taken away from your natural emotions. Storylines keep the process going by fueling the I-System. When you expand your awareness in a nonjudgmental way to recognize your I-System's activity, the I-System begins to lose its power, allowing your emotions to return to their natural state (executive functioning). You are now able to experience and express your natural emotions in a way that is best for you and the world, with your powerful self in charge.

Anxiety Reduction Tools

➤ Expand your awareness to recognize signs of emotions taken over by the I-System.

➤ Use nonjudgmental awareness to calm your I-System and restore your natural emotions.

➤ Bubble map the troubling items (thoughts associated with excess body tension) when your requirements are unclear.

➤ Befriend your anxiety symptoms.

MBB RATING SCALE: MASTER YOUR EMOTIONS

Date: _____

After using the tools in this chapter for several days, check the description that best matches your practice: hardly ever, sometimes, usually, or almost always.

How often do you...	Hardly Ever	Sometimes	Usually	Almost Always
Notice when your I-System has captured your emotions?				
Recognize the requirement driving the emotion?				
Bubble your maps to uncover additional requirements?				
Defuse requirements associated with emotions?				
Notice your active I-System creating your anxiety?				
Notice when your emotions are from your powerful self?				
Befriend your anxiety symptoms?				

List three emotions that were captured by the I-System:

_____

_____

_____

What were the requirements?

_____

_____

How did you befriend your anxiety symptoms?

_____

_____

CHAPTER 8

ACHIEVE HEALTH AND WELLNESS

Discover, Experience, and Apply

Discover how anxiety interferes with your health and wellness.

Experience how defusing requirements reduces anxiety and improves health and wellness.

Apply your anxiety reduction tools in your daily life.

Mind-Body Language

Mind-Body Bridging (MBB) action steps: Actions you take to achieve a goal that come from the two-part mind-body mapping process, and are carried out by your powerful self in the executive mode.

WHO'S IN CHARGE OF YOUR SELF-CARE?

Healthy lifestyle choices are becoming a top priority in health care systems around the world. Most people are knowledgeable about what is good for their health, but seem unable to follow through and make good choices. By now you know the truth about your I-System. When your I-System is in charge, not only will your anxiety symptoms increase, but your lifestyle and healthy choices will be limited.

Mary Mae, a married mother of two teenagers, was an "excess worrier" her entire life. Her everyday activities of preparing meals, getting the kids off to school, shopping, making plans for her husband's business trips, and calling her mother filled her mind with anxious thoughts and caused so much tension that her body screamed out in pain. She had seen physicians for a whole variety of symptoms and had received diagnoses of tension headaches, irritable bowel syndrome, anxiety disorder, insomnia, and hyperthyroidism, but all of her tests came back negative. Tranquilizers and sedatives only seemed to make her worry more about losing control of her life. She was so anxious about what problems her teenage son and daughter might have, that she paid little or no attention to her own health needs (proper diet, exercise, sleep, recreation, and so on).

After seeing a mind-body bridging therapist, Mary Mae discovered how her anxiety symptoms were being driven by her I-System and how her "twenty-four-hour worry train" was a result of the depressor/ fixer cycle and the accompanying storylines. What gave her the greatest relief was recognizing and defusing her requirements (*Nothing bad should happen to my children, The family should be happy, The kids should get excellent grades, Nothing unplanned should happen, My husband should be successful*). As she defused these requirements, it became clear that her I-System was driving her excess worries about everything in the world but herself. As her I-System quieted, she began to have more and more space to not only take care of her family appropriately, but to have time for her own self-care.

This chapter gives you the chance to put your powerful self in charge of your health and wellness, as you uncover even more requirements. Also, you will learn an effective new tool called *MBB (mind-body bridging) action steps*. You use the two-part mapping process to find actions you may take to reach a health and wellness goal that are free of the anxiety created by your I-System. When your I-System is at rest, you are in the executive mode, where you naturally achieve wellness and take care of yourself and your tasks without anxiety limiting your choices.

Gene, a healthy, upbeat executive, was diagnosed with prostate cancer at age fifty. His outlook on life changed, and he became anxious, irritable, and withdrawn. He was losing weight and not sleeping well. Despite the urging of his doctor, Gene put off getting medical treatment. His doctor finally referred him to mind-body bridging. When he did maps about his prostate cancer, he saw his many requirements and the ways his I-System used his anxious thoughts about cancer to control his life. Gene saw how his fixer kept him from admitting the reality of his cancer and kept his anxiety revved up: "It was my I-System that made me a victim, not my cancer." Gene's MBB action steps included working closely with his medical team to choose the right course of treatment. Gene stated, "I'm now a survivor rather than a victim."

WHO ARE YOU?

Do a Who Am I? map. Inside the circle, write the qualities that best describe who you are. After you have listed at least six qualities, outside the circle write the opposite of each quality, and connect it with a line. If needed, see the sample map that follows.

WHO AM I? MAP

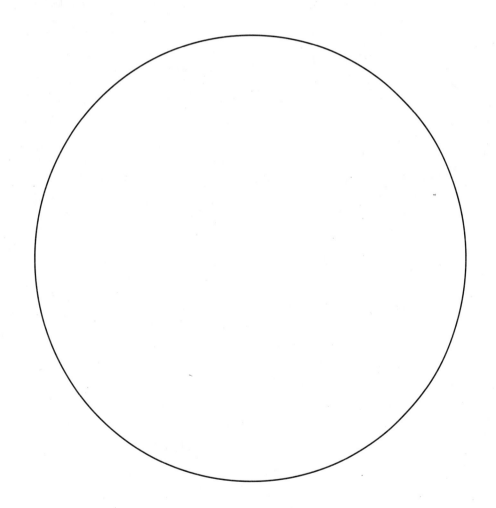

SAMPLE MAP: WHO AM I?

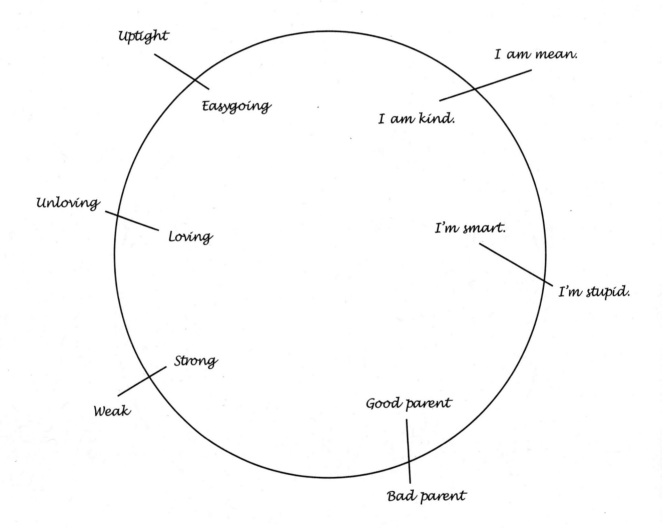

1. How does each quality *inside* the circle make you feel? Describe your body tension:

_____

_____

2. Describe how you act when you feel this way:

_____

_____

3. How does each quality *outside* the circle make you feel? Describe your body tension:

_____

_____

_____

4. Describe how you act when you feel this way:

_____

_____

5. Do the qualities inside the circle *really* describe who you are?   Yes _____   No _____

6. Do the qualities outside the circle *really* describe who you are?   Yes _____   No _____

Your I-System has you believing that the qualities inside the circle define you. Whenever you think you have any of the qualities outside the circle, your I-System tells you that you're lacking or damaged. Your actions then follow that feeling state. Your I-System wants to convince you that you are who you *think* you are. The qualities you listed are just thoughts about you, not you.

7. Use your bridging awareness practices and thought labeling, and review all the qualities on your map. What happens?

_____

_____

When you use your bridging awareness practices and thought labeling, you expand the circle to include everything on your map. When you aren't driven by your requirements, you are *everything*, which means you can have any quality on your map (even negative ones) without activating your I-System. When your powerful self is in charge, who you are is no longer limited by your I-System. Who you are is so vast, boundless, and ever-changing that your thinking mind can't grasp it. You are much greater than who you think you are. In this state of harmony and balance, you make the right choices to take care of yourself without anxiety.

CRISIS MANAGEMENT

1. At some time or other, everyone faces a crisis. Not only does a crisis create anxiety, but how you handle the crisis impacts your health and wellness. When you face any crisis, it's helpful to do a Crisis map. For this exercise, choose a crisis, big or small, in your life. Write the crisis in the oval. Take a couple of minutes to write around the oval whatever pops into your mind about how you can handle the crisis. Work quickly, without editing your thoughts. Your mind produces hundreds of thoughts each minute; the more open you are, the more insight you gain.

CRISIS MAP

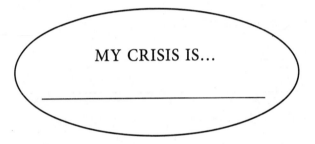

Body Tension: _____

A. Looking at your map, list the signs of your active I-System (requirements, depressor/fixer, storylines):

_____

_____

_____

_____

B. How would you feel and act in this mind-body state?

_____

2. Do this map using your bridging awareness practices. Write the same crisis in the oval. Before you start writing about how you can *handle* the crisis, listen to any background sounds, feel your body's pressure on your seat, sense your feet on the floor, and feel the pen in your hand. Take your time. Once you feel settled, keep feeling the pen in your hand and start writing. Watch the ink go onto the paper, and listen to any background sounds. For the next few minutes, write down whatever thoughts pop into your mind about your crisis.

CRISIS MAP WITH BRIDGING

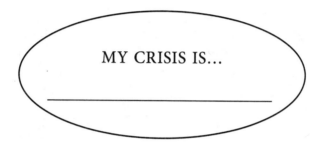

MY CRISIS IS...

_____

A. What do you notice that is different on this map?

_____

B. How do you feel and act with a quiet I-System?

_____

C. How will you defuse your requirements on the previous map when they come up during a crisis?

_____

_____

If you still have body tension that relates to the situation, find and break down the large requirement into smaller ones. Start by asking yourself, *What does that requirement look like?* Use your anxiety reduction tools to defuse those smaller requirements. When you face a crisis with a quiet I-System, your powerful self makes the best choices.

HOPES AND FEARS

1. Do a Hopes and Fears map. Take a couple of minutes to write around the oval whatever pops into your mind. Describe your body tension at the bottom of the map.

HOPES AND FEARS MAP

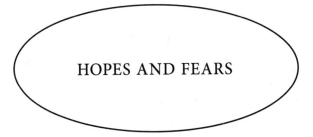

Body Tension: _____

A. Looking at your map, list the signs of your active I-System (requirements, depressor/fixer, storylines):

_____

_____

B. How would you feel and act in this mind-body state?

_____

_____

C. How would your reaction affect your health and wellness?

_____

_____

2. Do this map again. Before you start writing, use your bridging awareness practices. Listen to background sounds and feel your body's pressure on your seat, your feet on the floor, and the pen in your hand. Take your time. Once you are settled, keep feeling the pen in your hand as you start writing. Watch the ink go onto the paper and listen to background sounds. For the next few minutes, jot down any thoughts that come to mind about your hopes and fears.

HOPES AND FEARS MAP WITH BRIDGING

HOPES AND FEARS

A. What do you notice that's different on this map?

_____

_____

B. Defuse the requirements on your previous map. How did it go?

_____

_____

C. Do the fearful items on the previous map still create anxiety and impair your ability to care for yourself?   Yes _____   No _____

D. If your answer is yes, go back and use your bridging awareness practices and thought labeling on each of the items that still cause you problems.

E. Is your powerful self always within you, no matter what?   Yes _____   No _____

WHAT'S STILL HOLDING YOU BACK FROM ACHIEVING HEALTH AND WELLNESS?

1. List the most significant things holding you back from achieving your health and wellness goals. Do they include your genes, ethnic background, kids, lack of money, poor education, disease, trauma, or something else?

_____

_____

2. Do a What's Holding Me Back map. In the oval, write the most significant thing that's holding you back. Around the oval, write your thoughts for a couple of minutes without editing them. Describe your body tension at the bottom of the map.

WHAT'S HOLDING ME BACK MAP

Body Tension: _____

A. List your depressor/fixer storylines:

_____

_____

B. List your requirements:

_____

_____

C. Bubble your map, drawing a bubble around a thought that has a lot of body tension. Take a few minutes to write more thoughts around the bubbled item. Bubble any other troubling items to help you identify your health and wellness requirements.

3. Do this map again. In the oval, write the same problem that's holding you back. Before you start writing, listen to background sounds and feel your body's pressure on your seat, your feet on the floor, and the pen in your hand. Take your time. Once you are settled, keep feeling the pen in your hand as you start writing. Watch the ink go onto the paper and listen to background sounds. For the next few minutes, jot down any thoughts that come to mind.

WHAT'S HOLDING ME BACK MAP WITH BRIDGING

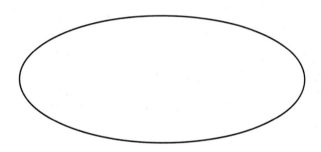

A. How is this map different from the prior map?

_____

B. What is really holding you back?

_____

C. Can you see that even if you have a serious disease, it is only your I-System that is holding you back from accessing your healing powers?   Yes _____   No _____

Accessing your innate healing powers to live your best life is what health and wellness are about and can only be done with a quiet I-System.

165

SELF-CARE GOALS

Now that it's becoming clear that anxiety impacts your choices in life, let's see who is in charge of your self-care goals.

1. Around the oval write some of your self-care goals (*Cut back on fried foods*) and your thoughts about them (*I have tried many times and always fail*). Write for a couple of minutes without editing your thoughts. Describe your body tension at the bottom of the map.

SELF-CARE GOALS MAP

SELF-CARE GOALS

Body Tension: _____

A. What are your depressors?

_____

B. What are your fixers?

_____

C. What are your storylines?

_____

D. What are your requirements?

_____

E. How do you take care of yourself in this state?

_____

2. Do this map again using bridging awareness practices. Before you start writing about your self-care goals, listen to background sounds and feel your body's pressure on your seat, your feet on the floor, and the pen in your hand. Take your time. Once you are settled, keep feeling the pen in your hand as you start writing. Watch the ink go onto the paper and keep listening to background sounds. For the next few minutes, jot down any thoughts that come to mind.

SELF-CARE GOALS MAP WITH BRIDGING

SELF-CARE GOALS

A. How is this map the same as or different from the previous map?

_____

B. Are any of the items associated with body tension?   Yes _____   No _____

C. For those items with body tension, do you recognize your requirements?

_____

_____

D. List the self-care goals that don't have associated body tension:

_____

_____

_____

To stop anxiety from influencing your health and well-being, simply quiet your I-System by defusing your requirements. This puts your natural executive-functioning self, rather than your I-System, in charge of your health and wellness.

DISCOVER MBB ACTION STEPS FOR SELF-CARE

1. Select one of the self-care goals listed on your previous map that was free of body tension. Write it in the oval. Next, take a couple of minutes to write around the oval your thoughts about what you are going to do to achieve that goal. Be specific. Describe your body tension at the bottom of the map.

SELF-CARE GOAL ACHIEVEMENT MAP

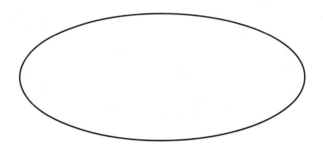

Body Tension: _____

A. What are your depressors?

_____

B. What are your fixers?

_____

C. What are your storylines?

_____

D. What are your requirements?

_____

_____

Did you see how your I-System grabbed a goal that used to be without body tension, created requirements about reaching your goal, and limited your success? Your active I-System will always create anxiety and muddle your path to health and wellness.

2. Do this map again using bridging awareness practices. Write the same topic in the oval. Before you start writing about how you are going to achieve that goal, listen to background sounds and feel your body's pressure on your seat, your feet on the floor, and the pen in your hand. Take your time. Once you are settled, keep feeling the pen in your hand as you start writing. Watch the ink go onto the paper and keep listening to background sounds. Write for a couple of minutes.

SELF-CARE GOAL ACHIEVEMENT MAP WITH BRIDGING

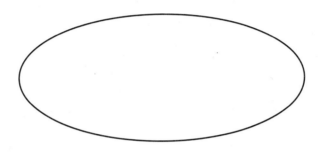

A. Circle those items *without* body tension. These are possible action steps.

B. Choose three of these items as the MBB action steps you plan to take for stress- and anxiety-free self-care. List them:

_____

_____

_____

You have used a two-part mapping process to separate the I-System's controlled action steps from the MBB action steps. You discovered that the items on your bridging awareness map that come without body tension and mind clutter are all MBB action steps that come from executive functioning. Choose the MBB action step that is the most important to you and put it into action today. For success in achieving your health and wellness goals, you need to do each action step with a quiet I-System. If you have body tension and mind clutter come up when you are doing your action steps, use your anxiety reduction tools to quiet your I-System. With the I-System no longer in charge, your choices now come from your executive mode, and the MBB action steps are done by your powerful self.

NOW IS THE ONLY TIME YOU CAN TAKE CARE OF YOURSELF

1. Do a Past, Present, and Future map. In the "Past" section of this map, take a couple of minutes to jot down whatever comes to mind about your past. Then describe your body tension. Next, in the "Future" section of this map, take another couple of minutes to write whatever comes to mind about your future. Describe your body tension. Finally, in the "Present" section of this map, take a couple of minutes to jot down whatever comes to mind about the present and, again, describe your body tension.

PAST, PRESENT, AND FUTURE MAP

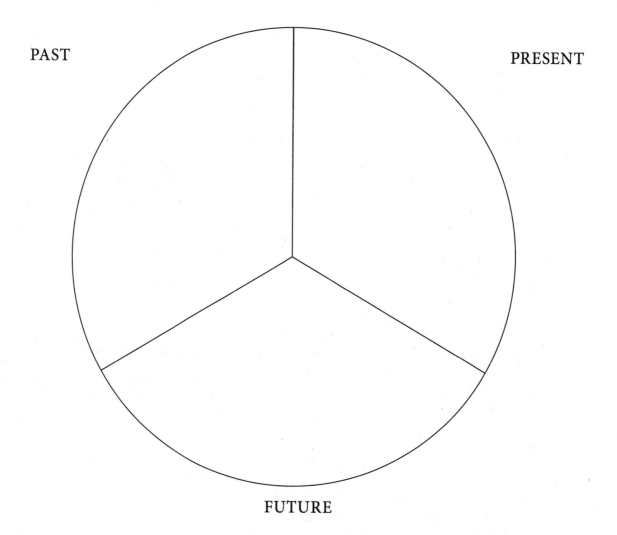

PAST

PRESENT

FUTURE

Let's think about this remarkable map.

A. The "Past" section of your map is full of storylines with themes like *My father was always ill* and *My friends always pushed me to party*. True or not, positive or negative, these stories create mind clutter; they tense your body and take you away from the present. When you recognize storylines in real time, notice that they take you away from doing what you need to do in the present.

What do you notice about the "Past" section of your map? List your storylines:

_____

_____

_____

B. The "Future" section of your map may have many of your hopes and dreams. Beside each item that brings body tension, write the requirements you can find. For instance, if the item that's creating body tension is *I won't be anxious*, the requirement is *I should not be anxious*. The I-System has taken hold of your naturally functioning thought, turned it into a requirement, and filled your body with tension and your mind with clutter. When thoughts about the future that are driven by the I-System come up in real time, note your body tension, find your requirements, and use bridging awareness practices and thought labeling to bring you back to the present.

List the requirements you notice on the "Future" section of your map:

_____

_____

_____

C. The "Present" section of this map shows what you currently feel and think. Look for signs of an active I-System, such as body tension, depressors, fixers, and storylines. Can you uncover your requirements? The I-System has taken stuff from your past and future to try to fix your damaged image of yourself. Look carefully for signs of the fixer and then find the hidden depressor. The depressor makes you feel broken and drives the fixer. You now know that the fixer can never "fix" the damage, because you aren't broken. You don't need fixing. The damaged self is caused by your active I-System, not what you have been through, and it limits your ability to fully live in the present.

List any signs of an active I-System you find in the "Present" section of your map. Also list your depressors, fixers, storylines, and requirements:

_____

_____

_____

2. Do a Present map. Before you start writing about the present, use your bridging awareness practices. Listen to background sounds and feel your body's pressure on your seat, your feet on the floor, and the pen in your hand. Take your time. Once you are settled, keep feeling the pen in your hand as you start writing any thoughts that come to mind about the present. Watch the ink go onto the paper and keep listening to background sounds.

PRESENT MAP WITH BRIDGING

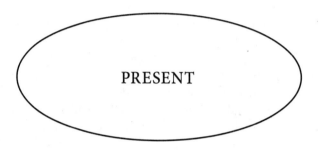

A. What do you notice about this map that's different from the "Present" section of your Past, Present, and Future Map?

_____

_____

B. Note how you would take care of yourself and your responsibilities in this mind-body state:

_____

_____

Being in the present is not being in a zone, nor is it a moment of enlightenment or a magical state of being. Your powerful self is always present right here, right now. When your I-System is calm, you are in the present, where your anxiety is well managed. Requirements take you away from your powerful self that is living right here, right now. If your depressor has you feeling *not good enough, bored, overwhelmed, lacking,* or *hopeless,* you have a hidden requirement that's pulling you down. On the other hand, when your fixer has you feeling jittery and anxious, and as if *enough is never enough,* you have a hidden requirement that's also taking over your executive functioning. When your I-System is active, look for your hidden requirement and use bridging awareness practices to come back to the present moment, do what you need to do, and take care of yourself right now.

APPLY THE TOOLS IN YOUR DAILY LIFE

Frankie, an overweight child, was bullied in school, and had only a few friends. In high school she became increasingly anxious about how her body looked. She started to restrict her eating and exercised constantly. Even when she reached her "ideal" body weight, she considered herself too fat, and just increased her exercise routine. As her preoccupation with her weight continued to grow, she began isolating herself from her friends, often missed school, and refused to attend school events. At first, Frankie's parents had been pleased at their daughter's weight loss, but soon they became concerned about her constant obsessing over her weight, her exercising, and her continuing isolation. They reached out to her school counselor.

Frankie's high school counselor referred her to a mind-body bridging group for teens. At first Frankie was not convinced that mind-body bridging did anything for her, but slowly she started using the anxiety reduction tools (awareness practices, thought labeling, and mind-body mapping). Whenever she had the thought *I'm fat*, she began to label it as "just a thought." Next Frankie would become aware of the background sounds around her. She was surprised at how calm she would become and at her ability to have control over her thoughts. Through her mind-body maps, Frankie discovered how her I-System's depressor and fixer were interacting. Her depressor thoughts and storylines were things like *I'm fat, No one likes me, My family doesn't love me because they keep trying to make me eat*. The fixer would respond with a wound-up, edgy body and thoughts like *Make myself thin, Exercise more, Eat less*. The depressor was driving her fixer and causing her anxiety as she tried to fulfill her many requirements connected to body image (*I should look perfect, I should be thin, My family should support me*). Frankie mapped her requirements and began to defuse them in real time. She discovered that when the excessive driving pressure of her fixer subsided, she could accept her body, eat appropriately, and be fit without anxiety.

After completing ten sessions of her mind-body bridging group and following through with her mind-body bridging assignments, Frankie is now a healthy high school sophomore with more friends, and is living her life without the anxiety driven by her I-System.

When you use your anxiety reduction tools, your powerful self, in the executive mode, is in charge of your self-care. With a clearer mind and calmer body, your decisions about your self-care are natural and the choices become clear. A unified mind-body state goes hand in hand with wellness.

Anxiety Reduction Tools

➤   Defuse requirements to allow proper self-care and support wellness.

➤   Uncover and use MBB action steps for healthy lifestyle choices.

MBB RATING SCALE: ACHIEVE HEALTH AND WELLNESS

Date: _____

After using the tools in this chapter for several days, check the description that best matches your practice: hardly ever, sometimes, usually, or almost always.

How often do you...	Hardly Ever	Sometimes	Usually	Almost Always
Know when your health and wellness are driven by your I-System?				
Notice when you are taking care of yourself and your I-System is at rest?				
Use your anxiety reduction tools to deal with a crisis?				
Recognize when requirements restrict your health and wellness decisions?				
Defuse requirements that get in the way of your self-care?				
Follow through with self-care MBB action steps?				
Notice that wellness and a resting I-System go hand in hand?				
Experience and express your powerful self in the present moment?				

List three situations where your I-System got in the way of your ability to care for yourself:

_____

_____

_____

List the requirements you were able to defuse associated with the situations above:

_____

_____

_____

List three self-care MBB action steps you are taking to ensure wellness:

_____

_____

CHAPTER 9

LIVE FREE OF ANXIETY

Discover, Experience, and Apply

Discover how the I-System stops you from living free of anxiety.

Experience the powerful effect of using your anxiety reduction tools regularly.

Apply your anxiety reduction tools in your daily life.

FACING THE FUTURE

The future is often uncertain and unpredictable. No one has control over what the future has in store for us. What you do have control over is who is in charge, your powerless self or your powerful self. When the I-System is in the driver's seat, challenges become full of anxiety as you are filled with a sense of powerlessness. When this happens, your anxiety symptoms are then likely to reappear. By making your anxiety reduction tools a part of your daily life, even when you face a full-blown stress-filled situation; you have the ability to do so in the executive mode, with your powerful self making the best choices.

Jack, a married copilot for a major European airline, developed a fear of flying in bad weather after a terrifying experience he had when flying in a storm. He would scan the weather reports for his upcoming flights and if he found bad weather, he would try to swap his flight with a fellow copilot. If he couldn't swap, he would call in sick. Jack's worry and anxiety began to interfere with his family life as those close to him saw how anxious he was. He tried many different techniques that made him a little less anxious, but his fear of flying in stormy weather continued.

When he began working with mind-body bridging, Jack learned how his depressor made him feel helpless, weak, and fearful. Then his fixer would go into overdrive, filling him with anxiety. If there was any possibility of bad weather, this depressor/fixer cycle would create ways to avoid flying. His bridging awareness practices, thought labeling, and mapping taught him how to calm his I-System. Jack began to worry less and his family life naturally improved. Jack continued mapping and created specific maps to address his fear of flying in bad weather, such as: Bad Weather Flying map, What If the Pilot Makes a Mistake map, and Traumatic Experience map. He identified the requirements *I shouldn't fly in bad weather, The pilot should be perfect, I should know I'll always be safe, I should always be in control,* and *Nothing bad should happen to me.* The turning point in his recovery was when he did the bridging part of his maps. On the first part of his maps he had clearly experienced that his I-System was creating mistrust of himself and others. When he did the bridging maps Jack gained access to his innate wellspring of healing, power, and wisdom. Now he trusts his true executive-functioning self's experience and judgment instead of his I-System's storylines. Jack is once again an all-weather copilot who enjoys his job.

This chapter brings together all your anxiety reduction tools so that you can effectively handle any challenge that comes up in life, free of anxiety. Also in this chapter, you will learn an advanced, rapid-fire mapping practice to find your hidden requirements, called *power mapping.* This free-association tool quickly expands your awareness of your requirements about a problem, situation, event, or person that is causing you to feel anxious. Without using your bridging awareness practices, you do map after map, just watching your switched-on I-System in action. When you power map, your I-System has free rein, but at the same time, your powerful self is still in the driver's seat. When you make a habit of power mapping, you experience firsthand that no matter what happens, your powerful self is in charge.

OVERTHINKING IMPAIRS THE QUALITY OF YOUR LIFE

1. List five situations where your overthinking bogs you down by creating anxiety. Find the requirement behind each event.

Situation	Overthinking	Requirement
Shaking hands with people.	*I can't stop my constant thoughts and worry about germs.*	*I shouldn't shake hands with people, I should not worry about germs.*
Leaving home.	*What if a window is open? What if I didn't lock the back door? The house is not secure.*	*My house should be secure, I should check and recheck all the doors and windows.*
Can't sleep the night before giving a presentation.	*I can't stop going over and over it. I'm making myself anxious and can't get to sleep.*	*I should give a perfect presentation, I should be able to sleep.*

The first step in dealing with a situation that is causing anxiety and bogging you down is to notice that *overthinking* is a signal that your I-System is on. Note your body tension—for example, tight shoulders or a knot in your stomach. Next, use your favorite bridging awareness practice (such as listening to background sounds or rubbing your fingers together) and find your requirement. To defuse a requirement, please remember to recognize that it's not the situation or even your anxious overthinking that is creating your distress; it's your I-System's requirement. Some requirements are easy to defuse, but if the requirement is hard to defuse, there may be other, related requirements you haven't found yet. Doing maps like the following ones will help.

2. Map the most troubling situation from the prior list where thinking too much has bogged you down. Write that situation in the oval (for example, *Going into a public restroom, Speaking at a meeting*). Around the oval, write your thoughts for a couple of minutes without editing them. Describe your body tension at the bottom of the map.

OVERTHINKING MAP

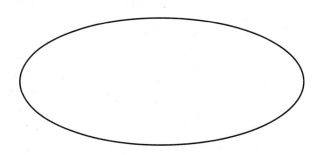

Body Tension: _____

A. What are your depressor/fixer storylines?

_____

_____

B. Find and list your hidden requirements.

_____

_____

C. Bubble your map, drawing a bubble around an item that has a lot of body tension. Take a few minutes to write more thoughts around the bubbled item. Bubble any other items filled with anxiety to help you find any hidden requirements.

3. Do the previous map again, writing the same situation in the oval. Before you start writing, listen to background sounds and feel your body's pressure on your seat, your feet on the floor, and the pen in your hand. Take your time. Once you are settled, keep feeling the pen in your hand as you start writing. Watch the ink go onto the paper and listen to background sounds. For the next few minutes, jot down any thoughts that come to mind.

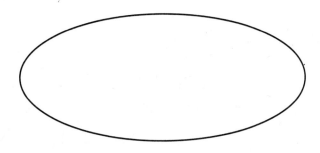

OVERTHINKING MAP WITH BRIDGING

A. What's your mind-body state on this map, compared to the previous map?

_____

_____

B. How would you feel and act differently if you were in this state?

_____

_____

C. Do you see that the real problem is not your thinking, but your I-System being turned on by requirements and driving your anxious storylines?   Yes _____   No

D. Describe how you will recognize and defuse your requirements in real time:

_____

_____

WHEN IS ENOUGH NOT ENOUGH?

Our I-System keeps comparing us to others. It tells us (by creating requirements about how we and the world should be) that we don't have enough of *something* (money, smarts, looks, education, or connections), resulting in excess worry and anxiety. Caught by the rules of the I-System, we respond with anxious thoughts and behaviors.

1. Think about a situation where you didn't have enough time, money, energy, attractiveness, talent, and so on that still brings up anxiety, body tension, and mind clutter. Now fill out the chart below.

Situation	Your Reaction	Requirements
Didn't have enough time to study for final exam.	*Got anxious and dropped the course.*	*I should have more time to study.* *I should be more prepared.*
Upcoming job interview.	*Couldn't sleep for days.* *Worried that they won't hire me.* *Uptight with anticipation.*	*I shouldn't have to interview.* *I should be acceptable.* *I should not be so uptight.* *They should hire me.*
Getting ready for a first date.	*Couldn't decide what to wear.* *Anxious if he will like me.* *Stomachache, worried all day.*	*I should look perfect.* *I should be at my best.* *He should like me.*

As long as your requirements are not defused, your I-System will control your life and create anxiety and jealousy. It is not what the other person has or what he or she is doing that is causing your difficulties; it's your I-System making you feel you will never have enough. The following maps will clarify the situation for you.

2. From the previous chart, choose the most anxiety-filled situation and write it in the oval below. Next, around the oval, write your thoughts about the situation. Write for a couple of minutes.

NOT ENOUGH MAP

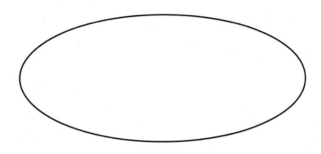

A. What is your body tension and how does it progress?

_____

B. What are your depressors?

_____

C. What are your fixers?

_____

D. What are your storylines?

_____

E. List your requirements:

_____

_____

F. Bubble your map, drawing a bubble around a thought that has a lot of body tension. Take a few minutes to write more thoughts around the bubbled item. Bubble any other troubling items.

3. Do this map again using bridging awareness practices. Write the same anxiety-filled situation in the oval. Before you continue writing, listen to background sounds and feel your body's pressure on your seat, your feet on the floor, and the pen in your hand. Take your time. Once you are settled, keep feeling the pen in your hand as you start writing. Watch the ink go onto the paper and keep listening to background sounds. For the next few minutes, jot down any thoughts that come to mind about the situation.

NOT ENOUGH MAP WITH BRIDGING

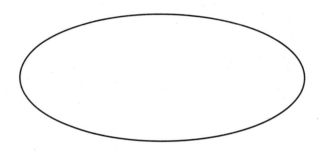

A. What do you notice that is different on this map?

_____

B. How do you act when your I-System is switched off?

_____

C. How will you defuse your requirements on the previous map when the situation arises again?

_____

_____

After doing the bridging map, if you still have body tension and feel you may have a hard time when the situation comes up again, use the following information about power mapping to find those stubbornly hidden requirements. Power mapping is only for people who have had success with using mind-body bridging practices in their daily lives. Use power mapping when your active I-System is hard to handle, such as when you have anxiety symptoms that are not easy to resolve.

POWER MAP YOUR WAY OUT OF ANXIETY

Power mapping is an advanced tool that only works when you have a solid foundation of mind-body bridging practices and have had success in recognizing and defusing requirements. It is important to have at least twenty to thirty minutes of time to yourself when you power map.

1. To power map, sit down with a pen and pad of paper. In the center of the paper, write the issue that troubles you the most (for example, *I have to get on a plane*). Draw an oval around that issue and quickly jot down whatever thoughts come to mind. Let your I-System run wild as you write. Don't use your bridging awareness practices, don't try to reduce your anxiety, and don't try to solve the issue. All you have to do is watch your I-System in action. When you have completed the map, write down your body tension at the bottom of the page.

2. Now take the most anxiety-filled thought from the map you just did, write it in an oval on another piece of paper, and begin mapping that thought. When you finish, write down your body tension at the bottom of the page. Repeat this process by taking the most anxiety-filled thought on one map and making it the topic of the next map. Make map after map after map. Map for as long as it takes, until your I-System quiets and your anxiety naturally decreases. Look over your maps for requirements you were not previously aware of. Those requirements were switching on your I-System and fueling your anxiety.

3. Review your series of maps and note how your body tension eventually reduces as your anxiety recedes. It's not possible to have anxiety without body tension.

When you power map, your I-System is on, but your powerful self remains in charge as you keep mapping. Let your I-System run free as you jot down your thoughts, emotions, and body tension. As time goes on, you will see that your I-System will, over time, run out of steam as you keep mapping. You are finding your hidden requirements while exhausting your I-System. This shows you that you can deal with those impulses and mental pressures, and your body tension, without having anxiety.

How did it go?

_____

_____

_____

_____

We all have an I-System and will never be rid of it. It's there to remind you of when you are off course (figure 2.1). It's your friend and your compass, telling you that you are not functioning in the executive mode. Power mapping shows you that no matter how intense your I-System is, you can always be the boss of your I-System without anxiety.

COMPETE WITHOUT ANXIETY

Everyone has a natural competitive nature and a drive to excel. When your I-System takes hold of this competitive spirit, it distorts your ambitions, creates anxiety, and affects your performance. When competition is pushed by the fixer, a friendly game can turn into a battle where no prisoners are taken, a simple conversation can develop into one-upmanship, losing ten pounds becomes a do-or-die struggle, and money equals self-worth. But since your depressor never approves, it drains your self-esteem, and no success will ever make you feel like a winner. The I-System also stifles your natural competitive spirit and inhibits you from expressing your powerful self in activities.

1. Think back to a competitive situation and what happened. Recognize your underlying requirements.

Competitive Situation	Your Behavior	Requirements
Women's Club election.	Excited, worried about who will vote for me. Only felt free to campaign after I did map.	I should be elected president.
Wanted to be the most attractive at the Holiday Ball.	Bought a great red dress, but was afraid to wear it. Wore last year's black dress.	I should be the sexiest.
I bogeyed the last nine holes when playing golf.	As it kept getting worse, I started shaking and felt like a loser.	I should play great golf.

When in a competitive situation, notice the early signs of your I-System: an urgent pressure to win, exaggerated storylines of losing, poor concentration, and mistakes. Remember that it's not the situation or even your competitive nature that is causing your anxiety-filled reactions; it's your requirements. When you don't defuse your requirement, it always has the power to inhibit your performance and create anxiety. Even if you do win, the anxiety associated with that requirement has kept you from competing at your best. Once recognized, some requirements are easy to defuse, but if the requirement is hard to defuse, realize that there are other, related requirements that you haven't found yet. Defusing your requirements frees up your drive to excel.

2. From the prior list, choose the competitive situation that created the most tension and anxiety. Write it in the oval. Around the oval, write your thoughts about this situation for a couple of minutes, without editing them.

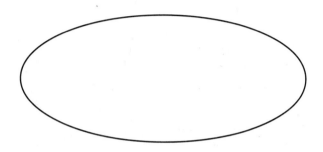

COMPETITION MAP

A. List your body tension and its progression:

_____

B. What are your depressor and fixer doing?

_____

_____

C. Identify and list as many requirements as you can:

_____

_____

_____

_____

D. How do you act in this state?

_____

Even if you win, the requirements on this map that are not defused will limit you.

3. Do the map again, writing the same competitive situation in the oval. Before you continue writing, listen to background sounds and feel your body's pressure on your seat, your feet on the floor, and the pen in your hand. Take your time. Once you are settled, keep feeling the pen in your hand as you start writing. Watch the ink go onto the paper and listen to background sounds. For the next few minutes, jot down any thoughts that come to mind.

COMPETITION MAP WITH BRIDGING

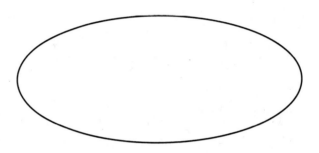

A. What's your mind-body state after bridging, and how do you act in this state?

_____

_____

B. How are you going to defuse the remaining requirements on your prior map?

_____

_____

Win, lose, or draw, defusing requirements means you win by having your powerful self, functioning in the executive mode, in charge.

CLARIFYING SUCCESS

Now that you have reduced your I-System's control and can deal with life with your powerful self in charge, let's move on to goals.

1. Write around the oval your thoughts about your personal goals for success. Write for a couple of minutes without editing your thoughts. Describe your body tension at the bottom of the map.

GOALS MAP

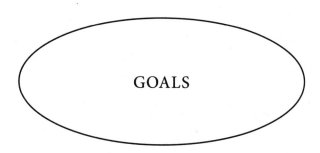

Body Tension: _____

What's your active I-System still doing?

A. What are your depressors?

_____

B. What are your fixers?

_____

C. What are your storylines?

_____

D. What are your requirements?

_____

Defusing these requirements is the path to goal fulfillment.

2. Do this map again using bridging awareness practices. Before you start writing, listen to background sounds and feel your body's pressure on your seat, your feet on the floor, and the pen in your hand. Take your time. Once you are settled, keep feeling the pen in your hand as you start writing. Watch the ink go onto the paper and keep listening to background sounds. For the next few minutes, jot down any thoughts that come to mind.

GOALS MAP WITH BRIDGING

GOALS

A. How is this map the same as, or different from, the one you just did?

_____

_____

B. Are any of the items on this map associated with body tension?   Yes _____   No _____

C. For those items with body tension, do you recognize your requirements? List them:

_____

_____

D. For those items without body tension, are your goals clearer?

_____

_____

DISCOVER MBB ACTION STEPS FOR SUCCESS

Let's put the pedal to the metal and see what action steps are necessary to achieve one of your goals.

1. Select one of the goals from your previous map that was *free* of body tension. Write it in the oval. Next, take a couple of minutes and write around the oval your thoughts on what to do to achieve that goal. Be specific. Describe your body tension at the bottom of the map.

ACHIEVING SUCCESS MAP

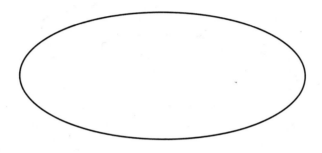

Body Tension: _____

    Let's look at what your active I-System is doing.

A. What are your depressors?

_____

B. What are your fixers?

_____

C. What are your storylines?

_____

D. What are your requirements?

_____

E. Your requirements are the obstacle that prevents forward motion. Can you defuse them?
Yes _____ No _____

2. Do this map again using bridging awareness practices. Write the same topic in the oval. Before you start writing about what to do to achieve your goal, listen to background sounds and feel your body's pressure on your seat, your feet on the floor, and the pen in your hand. Take your time. Once you are settled, keep feeling the pen in your hand as you start writing. Watch the ink go onto the paper and keep listening to background sounds. For the next few minutes, write any thoughts that come to mind.

ACHIEVING SUCCESS MAP WITH BRIDGING

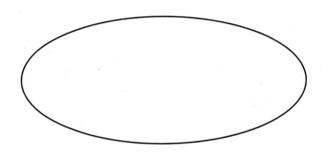

A. Circle those items *without* body tension. These are possible action steps.

B. Choose three of these items as the MBB action steps you want to take to achieve your goal. List them below and begin implementing them in your daily life.

Use this two-part mapping process to separate the I-System's anxiety-driven steps from the action steps you discover while in the executive mode (from your bridging awareness map). Remember that the items on your bridging awareness map with *no* associated body tension and mind clutter are all possible MBB action steps. Action steps that are conceived and implemented with a switched on I-System will always limit your outcomes. Use the two-part mapping process every day to navigate through life in the executive mode.

DO YOUR QUALITIES DEFINE OR CONFINE YOU?

Take a couple of minutes to think about your five most important qualities. Write one of your five most important qualities (for example, *trustworthy, hardworking,* or *loving*) inside each of the sections of the circle below. One or two words will do for each quality.

MY FIVE MOST IMPORTANT QUALITIES MAP

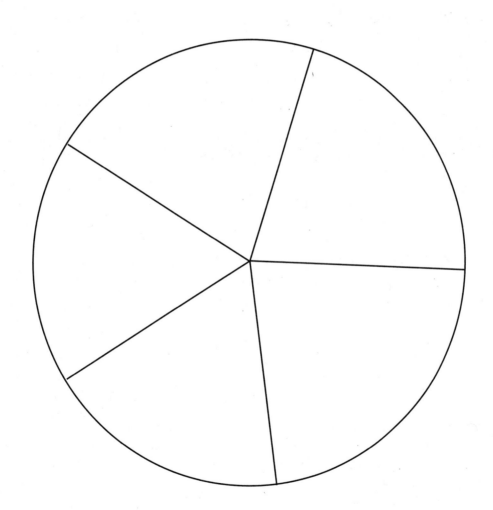

1. Look at your map and cross out the quality that's least important to you. What's your reaction as you imagine yourself without this first quality?

_____

_____

2. Cross out the quality that's the next least important to you. What's your reaction as you imagine yourself without this second quality?

_____

_____

3. Again, cross out the quality that's the next least important to you. What's your reaction as you cross out this third quality?

_____

_____

4. Choose between the last two qualities on your map and cross out the one that's less important to you. What's your reaction when you cross out this next-to-last quality?

_____

_____

5. Think about the last remaining quality. Cross it out. What's your experience now?

_____

_____

The levels of anxiety and body tension, and how hard it is to cross out these naturally functioning qualities, show how strongly the I-System confines you. It takes hold of your qualities and turns them into requirements. It's as if your goodness depends on meeting those requirements. Your reaction and body sensations when you were crossing out your qualities show how strongly your I-System tries to define you as a limited set of qualities. With a calm I-System, your natural powerful self is no longer confined to a narrow way of seeing yourself. In that executive functioning state, you, not your I-System, are the boss of how you live your life free of anxiety.

PREVENTING ANXIETY

1. Make a habit of using your mind-body bridging practices in your daily life, and do at least one map a day.

2. Use your body as a compass by noticing your personal and unique signs of body tension (stomach tight, shaky hands) that always come before your anxiety builds up. Then use all of your anxiety reduction tools and move into executive mode.

3. Use power mapping when you have stubbornly hidden requirements that create anxiety.

4. Live a full life with an I-System at rest.

APPLY THE TOOLS IN YOUR DAILY LIFE

You have now learned how to use all of your mind-body bridging anxiety reduction tools, and have mapped, recognized, and defused many of your requirements. These tools quiet your I-System so that you can manage any situation that comes up in your life without anxiety-driven actions. Remember, each moment that your I-System is in control is a moment filled with anxiety and powerlessness. When your powerful self, in the executive mode, is handling a situation, the choices you make guide you to your best life.

Anxiety Reduction Tools

➤ Use power mapping to map your way out of anxiety.

➤ Live life with an I-System that's at rest.

MBB RATING: LIVE FREE OF ANXIETY

Date: _____

After using the tools in this chapter for several days, check the description that best matches your practice: hardly ever, sometimes, usually, or almost always.

How often do you...	Hardly Ever	Sometimes	Usually	Almost Always
Listen to background sounds?				
Sense the sensation under your fingers when you take a drink?				
Experience gravity?				
Use bridging practices to reduce anxiety symptoms?				
Become really aware of your daily activities, like making the bed, eating, and driving?				
Hear the water going down the drain and experience the water on your body when you are showering or washing your hands?				
Use bridging to help you sleep?				
Use bridging to help you relax and stay focused?				
Notice body sensations as a sign of an active I-System?				
Realize that an active I-System is underlying your anxiety?				
Notice your depressor?				
Notice your fixer?				
Defuse your depressor?				
Defuse your fixer?				
Recognize storylines?				
Realize that requirements are causing your daily upsets?				
Recognize and defuse your requirements?				

Notice when the powerless self is in charge?				
Realize that the powerless self is a myth of the I-System?				
Recognize when you are in the executive mode?				
Notice when your powerful self is functioning moment by moment?				
Make daily mind-body maps?				
Use power mapping?				
Use your anxiety reduction tools?				
Live life in the executive mode, with your powerful self in charge?				

MBB QUALITY OF LIFE GAUGE

Date: _____

Only do this gauge when you have made a habit of using the anxiety reduction tools from this workbook in your life. Please compare your scores with those from the quality of life gauges in chapters 1 and 4. This gauge lets you measure your progress and keep track of your life-changing experience.

Over the past seven days, how did you do in these areas?

Circle the number under your answer.	Not at all	Several days	More than half the days	Nearly every day
1. I've had positive interest and pleasure in my activities.	0	1	3	5
2. I've felt optimistic, excited, and hopeful.	0	1	3	5
3. I've slept well and woken up feeling refreshed.	0	1	3	5
4. I've had lots of energy.	0	1	3	5
5. I've been able to focus on tasks and use self-discipline.	0	1	3	5
6. I've stayed healthy, eaten well, exercised, and had fun.	0	1	3	5
7. I've felt good about my relationships with my family and friends.	0	1	3	5
8. I've been satisfied with my accomplishments at home, work, or school.	0	1	3	5
9. I've been comfortable with my financial situation.	0	1	3	5
10. I've felt good about the spiritual base of my life.	0	1	3	5
11. I've been satisfied with the direction of my life.	0	1	3	5
12. I've felt fulfilled, with a sense of well-being and peace of mind.	0	1	3	5

Score Key: Column Total   ____   ____   ____   ____

0–15 . . . . Poor

16–30 . . . . Fair   Total Score _____

31–45 . . . . Good

46 and above . . . . Excellent

CONCLUSION

The design of this book is based on over a decade of research and clinical experience and is specifically adapted for individuals with all types of anxiety. Each mind-body bridging map is uniquely you. The appendixes of this book contain a two-part mapping template you can use for your daily ongoing mapping practice. Mapping gives you insight into what is happening in your life right here, right now. Remember, when you use your anxiety reduction tools, your inner power, wisdom, and beauty flow into your everyday life.

Anxiety Reduction Tools

CHAPTER 1

➢ Recognize when your I-System is active or inactive.

➢ Thought labeling.

➢ Bridging awareness practices:

· Awareness of the background sounds

· Awareness of what you are touching

· Awareness of colors, facial features, shapes

· Awareness of your body sensations

CHAPTER 2

➢ Create two-part mind-body maps every day and again whenever you begin to feel anxious.

➢ Discover requirements that activate your I-System.

➢ Recognize requirements to quiet your I-System.

➢ Use your body as a compass by befriending your body.

CHAPTER 3

➢ Recognize the depressor's activity.

➢ Become aware of your storylines.

➢ Defuse the depressor.

CHAPTER 4

➢ Defuse the fixer.

➤ Recognize the depressor/fixer cycle.

➤ Convert fixer activity into executive functioning.

CHAPTER 5

➤ Defuse your requirements for others and for situations.

CHAPTER 6

➤ Defuse your requirements for yourself.

➤ Defuse your requirements for your relationships.

➤ Mirror mapping.

CHAPTER 7

➤ Expand your awareness to recognize signs of emotions taken over by the I-System.

➤ Use your power of awareness to calm your I-System to restore your natural emotions.

➤ Bubble map the troubling items (thoughts associated with excess body tension) when your requirements are unclear.

➤ Befriend your anxiety symptoms.

CHAPTER 8

➤ Defuse requirements to allow proper self-care and support wellness.

➤ Uncover and use MBB action steps for healthy lifestyle choices.

CHAPTER 9

➤ Use power mapping to map your way out of anxiety.

➤ Live life with an I-System that's at rest.

Congratulations on completing this workbook! You have gained a unique freedom: the ability to live your life in the executive-functioning mode with an I-System at rest. With the anxiety reduction tools you have learned in this workbook, you can now live your best life with your natural powerful self in charge.

MIND-BODY BRIDGING
DAILY MAPPING GUIDE

1. Choose a mapping topic and write it in the oval. It may be as simple as "What's on My Mind?" or as specific as a certain troubling, anxiety-filled situation. Next, take a couple of minutes to write around the oval your thoughts about that topic. Be specific. Describe your body tension at the bottom of the map.

CHOOSE YOUR TOPIC MAP

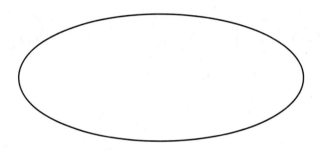

Body Tension: _____

Look at what your active I-System is doing.

A. What are your depressors?

_____

B. What are your fixers?

_____

C. What are your storylines?

_____

D. What are your requirements?

_____

E. How do you act in this mind-body state?

_____

2. Do this map again using bridging awareness practices. Write the same topic in the oval. Before you start writing about the topic, listen to background sounds and feel your body's pressure on your seat, your feet on the floor, and the pen in your hand. Take your time. Once you are settled, keep feeling the pen in your hand as you start writing. Watch the ink go onto the paper, and keep listening to background sounds. Write for a couple of minutes.

CHOOSE YOUR TOPIC MAP WITH BRIDGING

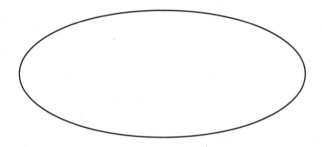

A. How is this map the same as or different from the previous one?

_____

_____

B. How do you act in this mind-body state?

_____

_____

C. Are you able to defuse the requirement on the previous map?

_____

_____

Remember, it's either your powerless self or your powerful self in the driver's seat. You choose.

APPENDIX B

MIND-BODY LANGUAGE

CHAPTER 1:

I-System: Each of us has an I-System, and it's either active (on) or resting (off). When it's on, it creates anxiety. You know the I-System is on when your mind is cluttered with spinning thoughts, your body is tense, your awareness contracts, and your mental and physical functioning is impaired. It's called the I-System because it prompts you to falsely identify with the spinning thoughts and the physical distress it causes.

Powerful self: How you think, feel, see the world, and act when your I-System is resting. Your powerful self always functions in the executive mode where your mind and body work in harmony, as a healing unit.

Mind-body bridging: When you use the tools in this workbook, you form a bridge from your active I-System, which can cause anxiety flare-ups, to your powerful self in the executive mode, which handles daily life in a smooth and healthy way.

CHAPTER 2:

Requirements: Thoughts made into mental rules by your I-System that tell how you and the world should be in each moment. When your I-System rules are broken you become fearful and full of anxiety.

Recognize requirements: When you become clearly aware that *your requirement*, not the events around you, is making your I-System active, you function in the self-healing executive mode.

CHAPTER 3:

Powerless self: How you think, feel, see the world, and act when your I-System is active. Life is overwhelming, your executive functioning is impaired, and you struggle to control your anxiety.

Depressor: A part of the I-System that takes your natural negative thoughts and self-talk (things you say to yourself) and creates body tension and mind clutter. It makes you feel weak, powerless, and vulnerable, setting the stage for your anxiety symptoms.

Storyline: Thoughts that your I-System spins into stories (true or not) that keep your I-System going, create anxiety, and pull you away from what you are presently doing.

Defusing the depressor: When you become clearly aware that your negative thoughts are "just thoughts," you reduce the power of the depressor. This allows your mind-body to start healing from the mental and physical distress (anxiety) caused by the I-System.

CHAPTER 4:

Fixer: The depressor's partner that drives your anxiety-filled behaviors with overactive, never-ending thoughts of how to fix yourself and the world.

Defusing the fixer: When you become clearly aware (at the time you are doing something) that your fixer is active and use your anxiety reduction tools, you take away the fixer's power. Right away, you feel a shift from a stressful, anxiety-filled state to one with a ready and relaxed mind and body. You can now calmly take care of yourself and whatever you have to do in the executive mode.

Depressor/fixer cycle: These I-System partners create a vicious cycle, keeping the I-System going and causing your anxiety symptoms.

CHAPTER 5:

Defusing requirements: When you use all your anxiety reduction tools, you handle a situation that used to make you anxious (turn on your I-System) with a ready and relaxed mind-body free of anxiety. Even when the I-System's picture of how you and the world should be is not fulfilled, the requirement is powerless to turn on your I-System and cause anxiety.

CHAPTER 8:

Mind-Body Bridging (MBB) action steps: Actions you take to achieve a goal that come from the two-part mind-body mapping process, and are carried out by your powerful self in the executive mode.

REFERENCES

Beck, J. S. 1995. *Cognitive Therapy: Basics and Beyond*. New York: Guilford.

Block, S. H., and C. B. Block. 2007. *Come to Your Senses: Demystifying the Mind-Body Connection*. 2nd ed. New York: Atria Books/Beyond Words Publishing.

Block, S. H., and C. B. Block. 2010. *Mind-Body Workbook for PTSD: A 10-Week Program for Healing After Trauma*. Oakland, CA: New Harbinger Publications.

Block, S. H., and C. B. Block. 2012. *Mind-Body Workbook for Stress: Effective Tools for Lifelong Stress Reduction and Crisis Management*. Oakland, CA: New Harbinger Publications.

Block, S. H., and C. B. Block. 2013. *Mind-Body Workbook for Anger: Effective Tools for Anger Management and Conflict Resolution*. Oakland, CA: New Harbinger Publications.

Block, S. H., S. H. Ho, and Y. Nakamura. 2009. "A Brain Basis for Transforming Consciousness with Mind-Body Bridging." Paper presented at Toward a Science of Consciousness conference, June 12, at Hong Kong Polytechnic University, Hong Kong, China, Abstract 93.

Boly, M., C. Phillips, E. Balteau, C. Schnakers, C. Degueldre, G. Moonen, et al. 2008. "Consciousness and Cerebral Baseline Activity Fluctuations." *Human Brain Mapping* 29 (7): 868-74.

Boly, M., C. Phillips, L. Tshibanda, A. Vanhaudenhuyse, M. Schabus, T. T. Dang-Vu, G. Moonen, R. Hustinx, P. Maquet, and S. Laureys. 2008. "Intrinsic Brain Activity in Altered States of Consciousness: How Conscious Is the Default Mode of Brain Function?" *Annals of the New York Academy of Sciences* 1129: 119-29.

Dutton, D. G., and D. J. Sonkin. 2002. *Intimate Violence: Contemporary Treatment Innovations*. Binghamton, NY: The Haworth Maltreatment and Trauma Press.

Hayes, S. 2005. *Get Out of Your Mind and Into Your Life: The New Acceptance and Commitment Therapy.* (ACT). Oakland, CA: New Harbinger Publications.

Lee, M. Y., A. Uken, and J. Sebold. 2004. "Accountability for Change: Solution-Focused Treatment with Domestic Violence Offenders." *Families in Society* 85 (4): 463–76.

Linehan, M. M. 1993. *Cognitive Behavioral Therapy for Borderline Personality Disorder.* New York: Guilford.

Lipschitz, D. L., R. Kuhn, A. Y. Kinney, G. W. Donaldson, Y. Nakamura. Forthcoming. "Reduction in Salivary Alpha-Amylase Levels Following Mind-Body Interventions in Cancer Survivors." *Psychoneuroendocrinology.*

Nakamura, Y., D. L. Lipschitz, R. Kuhn, A. Y. Kinney, and G. W. Donaldson. 2013. "Investigating Efficacy of Two Brief Mind-Body Intervention Programs for Managing Sleep Disturbance in Cancer Survivors: A Pilot Randomized Controlled Trial." *Journal of Cancer Survivorship* 7 (2): 165-82.

Nakamura, Y., D. L. Lipschitz, R. Landward, R. Kuhn, and G. West. 2011. "Two Sessions of Sleep-Focused Mind-Body Bridging Improve Self-Reported Symptoms of Sleep and PTSD in Veterans: A Pilot Randomized Controlled Trial." *Journal of Psychosomatic Research* 70 (4): 335-345.

Rosenberg, M. S. 2003. "Voices from the Group: Domestic Violence Offenders' Experience of Intervention." *Journal of Aggression, Maltreatment, and Trauma* 7 (1–2): 305–17.

Tollefson, D. R., K. Webb, D. Shumway, S. H. Block, and Y. Nakamura. 2009. "A Mind-Body Approach to Domestic Violence Perpetrator Treatment: Program Overview and Preliminary Outcomes." *Journal of Aggression, Maltreatment, and Trauma* 18 (1):17-45.

Weissman, D. H., K. C. Roberts, K. M. Visscher, and M. G. Woldorff. 2006. "The Neural Bases of Momentary Lapses in Attention." *Nature Neuroscience* 9 (7): 971-78.

Williams, M., J. Teasdale, Z. Segal, J. Kabat-Zinn. 2007. *The Mindful Way Through Depression.* New York: Guilford.

Stanley H. Block, MD, is adjunct professor of psychiatry at the University of Utah School of Medicine, and a board-certified psychiatrist and psychoanalyst. He is a consultant on the medical staff at US Army and Veterans Administration Hospitals. He lectures and consults with treatment centers worldwide and is coauthor of *Mind-Body Workbook for Stress, Mind-Body Workbook for PTSD, Mind-Body Workbook for Anger,* and *Come to Your Senses*. He and his wife, Carolyn Bryant Block, live in Copalis Beach, WA. Find out more about his work online at mindbodybridging.com.

Carolyn Bryant Block is coauthor of *Bridging the I-System, Come to Your Senses, Mind-Body Workbook for PTSD, Mind-Body Workbook for Stress,* and *Mind-Body Workbook for Anger*. She is the codeveloper of mind-body bridging.

Andrea A. Peters is an educator certified in mind-body bridging. She guided the organizational development of mind-body bridging material.

FROM OUR PUBLISHER—

As the publisher at New Harbinger and a clinical psychologist since 1978, I know that emotional problems are best helped with evidence-based therapies. These are the treatments derived from scientific research (randomized controlled trials) that show what works. Whether these treatments are delivered by trained clinicians or found in a self-help book, they are designed to provide you with proven strategies to overcome your problem.

Therapies that aren't evidence-based—whether offered by clinicians or in books—are much less likely to help. In fact, therapies that aren't guided by science may not help you at all. That's why this New Harbinger book is based on scientific evidence that the treatment can relieve emotional pain.

This is important: if this book isn't enough, and you need the help of a skilled therapist, use the following resources to find a clinician trained in the evidence-based protocols appropriate for your problem. And if you need more support—a community that understands what you're going through and can show you ways to cope—resources for that are provided below, as well.

Real help is available for the problems you have been struggling with. The skills you can learn from evidence-based therapies will change your life.

Matthew McKay, PhD
Publisher, New Harbinger Publications

**If you need a therapist, the following organization
can help you find a therapist trained in cognitive behavioral therapy (CBT).**

The Association for Behavioral & Cognitive Therapies (ABCT) Find-a-Therapist service offers a list of therapists schooled in CBT techniques. Therapists listed are licensed professionals who have met the membership requirements of ABCT and who have chosen to appear in the directory.
Please visit www.abct.org and click on *Find a Therapist*.

**For additional support for patients, family, and friends,
please contact the following:**

Anxiety and Depression Association of American (ADAA)
please visit www.adaa.org

National Alliance on Mental Illness (NAMI)
please visit www.nami.org

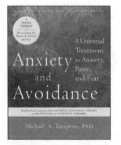